HIP
HOTELS

BUDGET

HERBERT YPMA

HIP
HOTELS

BUDGET

with 512 illustrations, 411 in color

Thames & Hudson

introduction

What do we look for in travel? Adventure? Escape? Fantasy? Probably a combination of all these. In short, we want an experience – a memorable experience. What good is going away, after all, if you don't come back with at least a few dinner parties'-worth of tall tales.

The surprise is that the most fantastic hotel experiences do not necessarily come only at the highest prices. This is not as unlikely as it sounds. A mud kasbah in the Sahara Desert, a converted sponge factory on a Greek island, an old pub in the Australian outback, a Mughal garden in Rajasthan: more often than not, such unique hotels are the creation of people more concerned with sharing an experience with their guests than with founding a hotel business empire. They are enthusiasts for whom culture, setting, and old-fashioned hospitality take higher priority than providing the world's fastest room service or the fluffiest towels.

Many of these hotels also play a part in preserving historic architecture and landscapes. Whether we are talking about antique wooden cabins in Norway, a sixteenth-century city palace in Jaipur, or a machine-age power plant in Hamburg, what they have in common is that by being converted into places to stay, they have all been saved from potential destruction.

The only catch is the difficulty of finding them. For chances are, if a hotel is not that concerned with becoming the next Ritz, then it's not likely to have a high-powered PR department either. That's where this latest edition of *Hip Hotels* comes in: it presents an astonishingly diverse collection of *affordable* Highly Individual Places. Every one is just as outstanding as the hotels in previous volumes, but none of them will break the bank.

Nor are they restricted to out-of-the-way locations. There are aesthetically inspired offerings in Sydney, Paris, Amsterdam and Miami. Even in Singapore, where most hotels are aimed at – and priced for – the corporate traveller, it's refreshing to see one of the city's most avant-garde buildings marketed as a hotel for a younger, more creative crowd – those with a green not a gold American Express card. That's not to say it is cheap. At around $150 a night, the Gallery Evason is pricier than the book's $90 average, and considerably more than the handful of $35 sensations. But given its location, it still represents tremendous value. In fact in an age when we almost automatically equate design with expense, it's a very pleasant surprise to discover that real style does not *have* to command inflated prices.

the kirketon

Sydney these days is a very modern town. There's a trendy café with bentwood chairs and polished aluminium tables on practically every corner, the city centre is full of immaculate all-white espresso bars, restaurants appear to be furnished almost exclusively with Danish design pieces, and the city's numerous lifestyle magazines seem to be forever trying to keep up with the latest designer grocery store or garage-turned-food-emporium.

What is this all about? Has Sydney always been this design conscious? The answer is a resounding *no*. In 1975 it was almost impossible to buy imported beer, wine or water, every corner had a pub not a café, restaurants served a choice of steak or fish with a prawn cocktail starter, and people didn't seem the least concerned what they sat on, Danish or otherwise. Stuffy, bureaucratic councils forbade outdoor consumption of any kind (food or drink) so there were no terraces or kerbside cafes. Worse than that, it was impossible to get a drink on a Sunday unless you went to the airport and pretended you were waiting for a friend's flight. The combination of colonialism, distance and a quasi-English pub culture (without the cosiness of English pubs) had produced an isolated, provincial environment.

So what happened? The simple answer is affordable air fares. All of a sudden every university graduate was taking a year off to travel. With typical Australian enthusiasm, they became the new Germans – you'd find an Aussie in the most unlikely and remote corners of the planet, and none ever went home empty handed – or rather empty headed, for what they took back with them were memories of all the bars, brasseries, cafés and restaurants they had seen abroad. And in a 'give-it-a-go' country, that's exactly what they did. First it was brasseries: whereas corner pubs had once had dining rooms, many now acquired brasseries. Next came the bistros: anyone who could afford the rent on a space big enough for five tables and twelve chairs started a bistro. Then things really started to accelerate as Italy's influence took hold, introducing words like *trattoria* to the local vocabulary and ushering in an awareness of coffee – real coffee. Sydneysiders rapidly mastered the difference between an espresso, a caffè latte, a cappuccino, a macchiato and a long black. Now there was no turning back. People were putting tables and chairs on the pavement – permission or not – pubs were working on their wine lists and staying open longer,

cafés were springing up in every defunct corner shop, new trendy food retailers were investing in stainless steel shelving, polished concrete floors and artful graphic design – and furniture importers were rubbing their hands in glee.

The past two decades have seen Sydney metamorphose from pleasant but sleepy colonial city into style powerhouse. These days it's impossible to open a copy of *Wallpaper* without finding at least a couple of pages devoted to places in Sydney. The city is hot, and for good reason. Unlike Europe and beyond, where the established way of doing things is as old as the road to Rome, Sydney has no conflict with a deeply ingrained culture. If any country was going to adopt modernity as its culture, it was Australia.

It was inevitable that this trend would reach hotels, as was the fact that at least one of them would be designed by Sydney architects Burley Katon Halliday. Directors David Katon and Iain Halliday have made a very successful career by providing the next step at each point of Sydney's fast-paced design evolution. The Kirketon's Saarinen tulip chairs and marble sidetables, Stelton pepper grinders and Bertoia chairs define a certain timelessness – a mature approach such as Sydney is now ready for. The brief was to create a small, beautifully styled and affordable hotel. At the same time proprietors Terry and Robert Schwamberg wanted a bar and restaurant that would keep the place alive and attract a clientele other than travellers. Burley Katon Halliday successfully followed this brief on all counts. Salt – the pared-down, Saarinen, stainless steel and granite restaurant on the ground floor – has earned a name as one of Sydney's best new establishments. The bar in the corridor and the red bar at the back are packed every night, and the hotel proper delivers just what it set out to do: it provides guests with an elegant and restrained interior environment without breaking the bank. All in all, it's a truly remarkable step up from the days of 'grill your own steak in the beer garden'.

address The Kirketon, 229 Darlinghurst Road, Darlinghurst, Sydney, NSW 2010, Australia

telephone (61) 2 9332 2011 **fax** (61) 2 9332 2499

room rates from A$220

the prairie hotel

They call it the back of beyond. This is the real outback, where everything is surrealistically distorted, where farms of 200,000 acres are considered to be on the smallish side, yet towns such as Parachilna count an official population of seven. Cattle are distributed one cow per square kilometre and the stockmen rely on planes, helicopters and motorbikes to keep track of their herds. A four-wheel drive is the most essential social tool (how else are you going to get to the pub?), and air-conditioning is the equivalent of heating in Scandinavia: life would be impossible without it.

There may be no more illustrative example of the back-of-beyond experience than the Prairie Hotel, or the Parachilna Pub as the locals know it. Parachilna is situated at the foot of South Australia's Flinders Ranges, the last geographical barrier en route to the middle of the continent. This is a vast empty land of red sand dunes, spectacular gorges, forests of dead trees, sparkling white salt beds that stretch to infinity, mountains that turn purple in the afternoon sun, and endless flat red plains punctuated by nothing more than the odd shrub. Almost every outback visual cliché exists within a thirty minute drive. This is where they filmed *Holy Smoke* (Kate Winslet and Harvey

Keitel stayed in rooms 11 and 12), while big-name director Philip Noyce of *Patriot Games* fame headed here to shoot his first film back in Australia, *Follow the Rabbit Proof Fence*. Using Parachilna as a base, every outback adventure is possible, from a picnic in a dry creek bed to a cattle drive on the prairie or a scenic flight over the Flinders Ranges. The fact that the hotel's own plane uses the road in front as a landing strip makes it even more convenient.

All in all, therefore, Parachilna is the last place you would expect to find fine cuisine. Yet the Prairie Hotel has earned an international reputation for its innovative use of bush tucker – or what they call 'Flinders Feral Food'. Where else in the world can you get an antipasto of smoked camel, char-grilled emu, smoked kangaroo and wild goat curd served with muntry fruit chutney? Or how about the feral mixed grill, with a goat chop, a kangaroo steak, camel sausages and wallaby shaslick served on a bed of mashed potatoes with homemade gravy? The front bar even serves a roo burger for lunch. Skippy on a bun? Try it and you will get over your reservations. Kangaroo tastes like a cross between venison and beef, smoked camel is almost the same as pastrami, and emu is like fillet of beef.

It wouldn't be the outback without at least one dry creek bed. Parachilna is a place straight out of a Slim Dusty song

Things aren't thrown away in the outback, they are recycled. Old biscuit tins get a new life as *objets d'art*

The Anchor of Hope sign is a filmset leftover from *Holy Smoke*, shot here with Kate Winslet and Harvey Keitel

Emu-egg omelette is occasionally on the menu. One egg feeds a dozen people – that's a big omelette

The most popular item on the front bar menu is the roo burger – minced skippy on a bun

Wattle leaf, gum nut, dried rooberries – wild bush food for those who wouldn't know how to find it for themselves

The intense summer heat produces mini-tornadoes that send the ubiquitous red dust swirling upwards

Owners Ross and Jane Fargher created a comfortable lobby in the space between the old pub and the new extension

The trains no longer stop in Parachilna, so the old station now houses the electricity generator

The outback is full of distortions of scale: for a town of seven, the Parachilna mail box is huge

Guest rooms at the Prairie Hotel are built partially below ground level for natural temperature control

Propping up the pub with a 'stubby' of beer in hand is a popular pastime in Parachilna

The stark Flinders landscape of red sand dunes makes it a favourite location with film makers

The severe terrain of the outback is the source of place names like Dead Horse Gap and No Name Creek

The galah, a beautifully colourful type of cockatoo, is a distinctively Australian bird

'Flinders Feral Food' – including wallaby, camel and emu – tastes surprisingly like continental charcuterie

The accommodation block to the rear of the pub seamlessly blends ecomodern design with outback vernacular

With its verandah and corrugated roof, almost nothing has changed at the Prairie Hotel since it was built in 1874

The unusual cuisine is not a gimmick – far from it. The fact is that Australia has wild camels (too many), kangaroos (too many), wallabies (too many) and emus (too many). And these animals need to be culled on a regular basis. Common sense says that if they are going to be killed they might as well be eaten. That's certainly what Jane Fargher thought, when she and her station-owning husband Ross took over the Parachilna Pub some ten years ago. And there is the added bonus that the meat of these animals is very low in fat and cholesterol.

But to dwell too much on the ingredients served at the Prairie Hotel is an injustice to the chef. The menu has great diversity, and there are many dishes that don't feature Australia's more graphic fauna. In any case, fascinating food and spectacular scenery were only part of Ross and Jane's agenda for their outback establishment. They were also intent on creating an architectural experience. Modern architecture is not exactly commonplace in the bush – which for Jane was all the more reason to pursue it. The accommodation, lying behind the typical stone facade, corrugated roof, and lace ironwork of the old pub, is a fine piece of ecomodern design. It was devised to provide a cooling system that would not consume vast amounts of energy. The solution was to dig the rooms into the ground. The surrounding earth acts as insulation while the interior space is made much more interesting. Each room is on two levels, a balcony where you enter and a cool, shady lower sleeping area. Bathroom and corridor are at ground-floor height, bedroom half a floor lower.

Still, few people spend much time in their rooms – not when there is the ever-changing spectacle of 'bush life' in the front bar. During the day it is frequented by local characters: stockmen, bushies, rangers, truckies, mineworkers and flying doctors. All afternoon they sit in the front bar looking out on the fence. When the blazing sun abates, they settle on the fence and look at the bar. Whoever said outback life is uneventful?

---

address The Prairie Hotel, CMB 109, High Street Parachilna, SA 5730, Australia

telephone (61) 8 8648 4844/4895 **fax** (61) 8 8648 4606

room rates A$100 (including breakfast)

w sydney

Woolloomooloo, the name of one of Sydney's inner harbourside districts, has always been my favourite Aboriginal word. But believe it or not, the fact that the hotel there is called W is a coincidence. W is the invention of the giant Starwood hotel group – a corporate effort to cater to the demands of a younger and cooler travel audience. There are Ws in New York, Los Angeles, San Francisco and Atlanta, and more are planned. But this was the first W outside North America. Doesn't that contradict the idea of a Highly Individual Place, you may ask? Is manufactured hip still hip? It depends. As with any chain hotel, a lot depends on the individual property. With such a unique setting as the Woolloomooloo Finger Wharf, the W Sydney was virtually immune from corporate formulae.

Built in the mid-1800s for loading wool onto ships making the passage back to England, the wharf sticks out like a long finger for almost a kilometre into Sydney Harbour. It's a huge, industrial-scale structure built entirely in wood – mighty beams of Western Australian Jarrah, a now protected species of rock-hard redwood that is unique to Australia. Even the crude mechanisms for loading the bales onto ships are still in place. The entire structure is a testament to the extraordinary strength and durability not just of the timber but of the way they used to build in Sydney – rough, solid, and above all big. Too big, in fact, to be used for anything else: with the advent of modern containerized shipping, this wharf and others became redundant. But instead of demolishing them, the maritime service board simply – luckily – opted to ignore them. It was all rather like the recent history of London's Battersea Power Station – every few years someone would dream up a half-baked plan for Woolloomooloo's timber peninsula; but it always came to nothing, and time moved on.

It took a catalyst as powerful as the 2000 Olympics to get things moving. Realization dawned that this lumbering giant might make a nice place to live. Harbour on all sides, a stone's throw from the city centre – *of course* it would be a nice place to live. Plans were drawn up to convert half to apartments and put the other half out to tender for a hotel. There was just one snag: the demand for the apartments, long before they were finished, was so overwhelming that the property developers halved the area originally allocated to the hotel. In fact that was a blessing in disguise. The new W, although still big, is not a place where guests would ever feel like numbers.

Completed just in time for the Olympics, the W at Woolloomooloo is what Sydney has needed for a long time – a hotel that encapsulates the entire Sydney experience: the harbour, the history, the modernity, the character, the food and the atmosphere. Once one of the most derelict and dangerous parts of town, Woolloomooloo has now become one of its most fashionable. There's a brand new marina nestling on one side of the wharf, with an entire half-kilometre stretch given over to cafés and restaurants. People sit outside under umbrellas taking in the weather and the view of Sydney's skyline and enjoying a relaxing lifestyle that is no doubt a vast improvement on that of a wool storeman.

It's heartening to see that the functional integrity of the building has been preserved in its redesign. It may be a popular place to stay and a hot location to eat, but the architecture and detailing remain intact inside and out. The hotel rooms, for instance, feature exposed beams, complete with the original iron-rod bracing system. Public areas such as the bar, lobby and restaurant have been placed in the centre of the massive building a bit like furniture in a doll's house. It looks good, but it also looks temporary, as if – were it to be required – all traces of this modern intrusion could be removed in a jiffy. Not that that's likely to happen: the hotel is incredibly popular. That's no surprise given its location, but there is also the fact that this mammoth manmade peninsula is big enough for lots of extras like a state-of-the-art gym complete with indoor pool for W guests, plus restaurants, bars, cafés and shops for everybody. And for guests who have to work, the centre, or CBD as they call it in Sydney, is only two minutes away.

Unbelievable, really, that just a decade ago there was only one reason to come to this part of town, and then only late at night, and preferably drunk – that was to stand outside a small caravan converted to a kitchen waiting your turn to order a legendary 'pie floater' from 'Harry's Café de Wheels'.

---

address W Sydney, 6 Cowper Road, Woolloomooloo, NSW 2011, Sydney, Australia

telephone (61) 2 9331 9000 **fax** (61) 2 9331 9031

room rates from A$257

waka gangga

Bali has some pretty places, some not so pretty places, and some heart-stoppingly beautiful places. The road that leads to the coastal village of Gangga shows you all three. From Denpasar airport you first travel through Kuta, the Balinese Costa del Sol: lots of shops, lots of uninspiring hotels, and lots of drunk tourists. A bit further along you reach Legian, home of some of the prettiest beaches and best surf on Bali. It's still over-developed, but far less abrasive than the Kentucky-Fried McDonald's culture of Kuta. Once past Legian, you are into rural Bali, a landscape of small villages, verdant rice terraces, palm trees and ornate Hindu temples. This is farm country, where people still work the land with ox-drawn ploughs, and families stand knee-deep in dark brown mud to tend to their rice crop. It's not a geography that one would normally associate with a resort – which is part of the beauty and fun of the Waka complex just outside the village of Gangga.

Waka Gangga is a hidden gem, a mysterious and mystical place that you would never find by accident. Locals describe it as a place of potent, primitive spirituality, and if appearances are anything to go by, they may be right. Impossibly green rice paddies framed by Bali's mountains descend to a seemingly

endless stretch of volcanic black sand beach where row upon row of undiscovered, unsurfed waves roll majestically in. The visual sequence is breathtaking: cloud-wrapped mountains, verdant cascading rice paddies, sparkling black beach, crashing surf. In the early morning, horses ride along the beach, and the odd Balinese fisherman stands waist-deep in the water to cast his net.

The architecture and design of Waka Gangga take this powerful natural beauty to another level. The first thing you see upon arriving is a large round thatched pavilion sitting on top of a platform of volcanic stone. This is Waka Gangga's dining room, and it sets the almost reverential tone of this extraordinary complex. With a nod to the architecture of the famous Tanah Lot temple nearby, it celebrates the site. Its raised position seems to suggest that one should feel honoured and privileged to be in such an incredible spot.

The inspiration for all this, the newest Waka experience, came, unusually enough, from the 1961 cult film *One Eyed Jacks*. Starring and directed by Marlon Brando, it tells the story of a gunfighter who retreats to a remote part of Hawaii to recover from a near-fatal injury inflicted by bad buy Karl Malden.

Each guest bungalow at Waka Gangga features an extraordinary outside bathroom with sunken terrazzo bath

Perched on its own pyramid of volcanic stone, the dining hut affords amazing views of the surf and the beach

Waka architect Ketut Siendana very skilfully blends Balinese tradition with contemporary trends

Faded teak benches on a discreet platform provide each bungalow with an interesting little space to escape to

Beautifully handcrafted mosquito nets – a room within a room – have become a trademark of the Waka experience

Eco-friendly privacy: each thatched guest bungalow is set on stilts in its own patch of worked rice paddies

In the film, Brando takes long solitary walks on a black-sand beach, eats potent health-giving food and recovers both spiritually and physically, returning to deal with Karl Malden (permanently) and ride off into the sunset with his daughter. The ending – courtesy of studio bosses – is typical Hollywood, but as inspiration the film has a lot of synergy with Waka Gangga.

Everything from the architecture, design, food and service has been geared to creating a soothing, nurturing, natural retreat in this amazing location. There's a massage centre immediately adjoining the fresh-water lap pool where guests can receive a rejuvenating Balinese massage while listening to the rhythmically crashing surf. The twelve very private and very spacious bungalows form a cascading arrangement down the stepped rice paddies that lead to the beach (two bungalows per terrace as a general rule). Waka Gangga is a dramatic mix of old and new, of traditional Bali and modern design, that never resorts to

clichés or nostalgia. The roofs are of indigenous *alang alang* grass thatch and the beds are cocooned in a canopy of intricate, handmade mosquito net. The minibar is hidden in a minimal streamlined cupboard of coconut timber and the light controls are built into an equally minimal coconut-wood bedhead. Bathrooms are open to the sky and the bath and washbasin are unexpectedly crafted from glass-specked terrazzo.

The design skills of architect Ketut Siendana, the catering skills of his brother Intut, and the management skills of brother Daysu bring expertise, youth and vibrancy to cultural authenticity. Their easy, funky mix of tradition and modernity is what makes Waka hotels so hip. Ketut and his brothers are pure Balinese. They pray a lot, they regularly attend Hindu ceremonies, they take their faith and their culture very seriously. But all three also happen to be completely fanatical about Harley Davidsons. Hindus on Harleys – that says it all.

address Waka Gangga, Banjar Yeh Gangga, Desa Sudimara, Tabanan, Bali, Indonesia
telephone (62) 361 416 256 **fax** (62) 361 416 353
room rates from US$125

waka shorea

I doubt that even the most dedicated Bali buff has been to Gobleg. Situated deep in the heart of Bali's central mountains, arranged along a ridge on their highest peak (at 3,100 metres), Gobleg is a one-motorbike town that takes in possibly the most spectacular panorama on the island, a bird's-eye view of an immense crater lake. This is Balinese alpine country: the weather is noticeably cooler and tourists are virtually unknown.

Gobleg is just one of the extraordinary places you will visit on the way to Waka Shorea. In fact the four-hour journey is almost as riveting as the destination. En route from Denpasar airport you will travel through both the least and the most densely populated parts of Bali. By the time you reach the entrance to the park, you will have essentially seen most of the island.

According to the map, Waka Shorea doesn't even exist. This northwestern tip of Bali, very close to neighbouring Java, is a national park and no resorts are allowed – except, that is, for one by the Waka group. Ketut Siendana and his brothers were invited by the Indonesian company that has a lease on all of the country's nature reserves to establish an ecologically sensitive resort here.

Shorea is a small compound specifically designed *not* to be noticed, much in the same vein as Amanwana, the tent village retreat on nearby Moyo Island. In fact even from a boat it's impossible to spot. Only when you are literally a few hundred metres from the wooden jetty do the guest bungalows begin to loom out from behind the eucalyptus and jacaranda trees that predominate in this area, in contrast to the palms and rice paddies that are so ubiquitous elsewhere. For this northernmost point of Bali is rather less tropical and lush – peculiar, considering that it is nearer the equator.

Even at the park entrance, your journey is not over. Next on the agenda is a transfer to a small blue-painted wooden fishing boat. A sea-going vessel this is not. The slightest chop on the bay that you must cross can turn the ten-minute trip into an adventure. What is most extraordinary is that the very same boats were used to transport all the building materials for Waka Shorea. The bricks, concrete, timber, pumps, generators, commercial kitchen, furniture – all came across in these large wooden dinghies fitted with an outboard. They had to, because although Waka Shorea is on a peninsula, there is no access road.

Shorea guests are the only people in this area. The rest of the wildlife is four-legged and hairy (including warthogs, deer and silver leaf monkeys) or colourful and wet (including live coral). According to underwater enthusiasts, this is one of the best diving areas of Bali, and Waka Shorea is equipped with an admirable assembly of gear and a full-time diving instructor. Back to nature may be a bit of a cliché, but at Waka Shorea it really does describe what's on offer. The resort is completely designed to enable guests to squeeze the most out of these extraordinary surroundings. There's always a boat ready to take you snorkelling on nearby Menjangan Island, or to a remote beach or the volcanic amphitheatre that frames the setting. From the deck of your little wooden punt, you are virtually surrounded by a spectacular group of five dormant volcanoes arranged in a sickle-shaped pattern.

The architectural inspiration came from the original Treetops Hotel in Kenya, and accordingly, wherever possible, the guest villas as well as the dining pavilion and even the massage centre were designed to jut out over the trees. As at other Waka resorts, there are beautifully crafted mosquito nets, indoor-outdoor bathrooms, and modern handcrafted furniture. The difference here is that despite the luxury and comfort, most guests spend every waking hour in the great outdoors. A dinner for two on the jetty, a picnic on a deserted beach, breakfast on the edge of a reef … every barefoot fantasy you can conjure is catered for at Waka Shorea.

Perhaps the most extraordinary quality of Shorea, and one that cannot be found anywhere else on this dreamlike island, is its complete sense of isolation. Bali has a generous selection of amazing locations, but no matter how spectacular or inspiring, there are always people around to remind you that this is a densely populated part of the globe. At Shorea can you truly fulfil your desert-island fantasy.

address Waka Shorea, Menjangan Island, Bali, Indonesia
telephone (62) 362 828 361 445/448   **fax** (62) 362 828 361 341
room rates from US$130

't sandt

Translated from Flemish, the name 't Sandt means 'The Sand'. How, you may reasonably ask, did a hotel in the centre of one of Europe's oldest (and hippest) cities end up with such a name? The answer lies in the long history of the site and the building. This was once a triangular stretch of sand right on the waterfront of Antwerp's busy harbour. According to municipal records the Duke of Brabant granted this piece of land (or rather sand) to the city in 1396. The harbour was already the commercial heartland, and construction quickly got under way. The building that is now 't Sandt has always housed some sort of trade or manufacture. First it was the customs duty offices, then for almost three centuries until the mid-1800s it housed the Ash Barrels soap factory (the name referred to the copious quantities of ash used to make green and brown soap). In more recent times it was occupied by the country's first banana importer, a fruit largely unknown in Belgium before 1912. By then, however, the property had long since lost its seafront location. Large pieces of land were filled in during the Napoleonic era to make more commercial space, and the Ash Barrels found itself one street back from the water.

Today the building's long historical journey has entered a new stage. 'T Sandt was opened just seven years ago, and it is one of the few interesting and individual hotels in Antwerp. Thanks to the city's newfound status as a European style hotspot, it is understandably almost always full. Anyone even vaguely familiar with contemporary fashion will have heard the names Ann Demeulemeester, Martin Margiela, Dries Van Noten and Walter Van Beirendonck. Antwerp, by no means the largest city in Belgium, is nonetheless the undisputed capital of the Belgian avant-garde – and not just in fashion, but also in interior design and food. It boasts some of the most unusual and creative boutiques and restaurants in Europe. Brussels may have the international community, but Antwerp has the edge.

Historically speaking, this is nothing new. Antwerp and Amsterdam have traditionally been the dynamic duo of the Low Countries. In the Golden Age of the seventeenth century, Amsterdam had Rembrandt and Antwerp had Rubens. Both cities were major ports and both gave refuge to the diamond cutters and dealers who were banished from their native Lisbon. As a result, Amsterdam and Antwerp became the two major diamond centres of the world.

These ornate market pavilions are directly opposite the entrance to Antwerp's Hotel t 'Sandt

From the private terrace of the penthouse, there's a splendid view of Antwerp's impressive cathedral

This enormous wooden wheel was used to haul goods in and out back in the days when this was a soap factory

The building may date back six centuries but, aside from their ancient beams, bathrooms are all brand new

The restaurant, decorated in what you might call 'Belgian beer bottle baroque', is one of Antwerp's best

T 'Sandt combines gentleman-proprietor's townhouse at the front and soap factory hidden away at the back

Trade brought wealth, and wealth brought patronage, in architecture, in extravagant town planning, and in art.

People often forget this heritage when they speak of Antwerp. Maybe they prefer to believe that the city's current prominence is a spontaneous creative flourishing that could happen to any city. Don't bet on it. Wander through the centre and you will see droves of elegantly dressed people; a seemingly endless choice of interesting restaurants hidden behind gingerbread-house facades; and an incredible variety of boutiques, cafés and beautifully presented patisseries lining all the old cobblestone squares. You don't need to be a historian to see that Antwerp's newfound success has deep roots.

Just as in Amsterdam, however, the standard of hotel accommodation lags dreadfully behind. Of course there are exceptions, including the magnificent De Witte Lelie. But it's expensive and only has seven rooms. Hotel 't Sandt is slightly less luxurious –

but only just – and it has seventeen rooms and a very popular restaurant, 't Zavel.

Architecturally speaking, 't Sandt is highly unusual. The building is split into two parts: the old proprietor's mansion in front with an ornate neo-rococo facade (a Louis Philippe imitation of Louis XV), and the rather larger former factory to the back. Some rooms have elegant historic detailing, while others are like lofts, and the courtyard garden has exposed steel beams. As you proceed from one room to another, the spaces change effortlessly from grand chic to functional industrialism. My favourite room is the Penthouse at the back of the former factory, which still contains the massive wooden wheel once used to winch goods in and out through the windows.

These days the business of Antwerp is more concerned with the export of banana-yellow couture than the import of bananas. It's welcome to see an old storehouse put to use as something other than yet another advertising agency office.

address 'T Sandt, Zand 17–19, 2000 Antwerp, Belgium

telephone (32) 3 232 9390 **fax** (32) 3 232 5613

room rates from 5,122 BFr

la aldea

Chile is a country of geographical extremes: one is Patagonia, the southernmost landmass on the planet (short of the South Pole), a wet, cold, wild and splendidly isolated landscape of glaciers, mountains, lakes and rivers. The other extreme is the Atacama, a hot, dry, volcanic plateau in the far north of the country. It is equally remote and untouched, but instead of ice and stone you get fire, salt and sand. Until recently, Patagonia was the better known of the two. Atacama, in terms of international exposure, is the new kid on the block. But with the advent of more affordable travel and a greater global awareness, Chile is no longer as remote a destination as it was. These days people really scour the globe for that exotic experience, and Atacama qualifies hands down.

The Atacama Desert is the driest place on earth. In the past hundred years, there's been hardly any rainfall at all, and if it wasn't for the oasis town of San Pedro de Atacama, it's doubtful whether this volcanic moonscape could sustain any kind of tourism. Its *altiplano* landscape combines the bizarre extremes of high altitude – 2,443 m (8,015 ft) – and desert. Yet despite all, the place is far from bleak. Stark, dramatic, imposing and empty, yes – but not bleak. This is an endlessly enthralling landscape: the vast dried-up salt lake of Salar de Atacama, for example, appears to stretch into infinity towards the snow-capped Andes; the haunting Valle de la Luna is a basin of rock-hard sunbaked clay impregnated with crystals of salt that glisten by moonlight; and the hundred geysers of Tatio inexplicably gush only from dawn until 10 am. Add to this archaeological monuments, churches, villages, and local craft traditions, and it's clear that there is no shortage of things to see or do. The Atacama plateau is an ancient crossroads between Bolivia, Chile and Argentina, with a 3,000-year history of habitation. Not every visitor opts to climb the nearby peak of El Toco (5,600 m; 18,400 ft) and certainly very few are crazy enough to attempt the ascent of the volcano Sairecabur (6,100 m; 20,000 ft; serious alpine experience required). But it's all there if you are inclined to adventure.

For those accustomed to having everything organized for them, the Hotel Explora is ideal: it was designed to showcase the Atacama wilderness as a comprehensive all-inclusive package. Mollycoddling, however, only comes at a price, and for those who would prefer to spend less and set their own agenda, the hotel La Aldea is perfect.

Architecturally, La Aldea is one hundred per cent the part. It looks like a cluster of indigenous shacks, with typical red adobe walls and ragged reed roofs – which was exactly the idea. Architect Bernardo Echaurren and his client Ricardo Quiros Nilo wanted a design inspired by ancient Indian settlements that would blend with the surroundings. The name means village, and the huts are arranged in a circle as in the traditional *aldea* to protect against the harsh climate. But it's not just the architecture that takes its design cue from the environment. Throughout La Aldea's interiors, the influence of the desert's pared-down beauty is evident. Floors are of plain wood or locally baked tiles, beds are covered in simple white cotton, wrought-iron candlesticks constitute about the only decorative detail, and the colour – the only colour – is the warm red and dappled orange of the clay used in the reed-framed adobe mud construction. No pictures mar the beautiful handcrafted inconsistency of the hotel's walls. Plain sisal matting in the

bathrooms continues the disciplined lack of adornment. But do not be concerned: this is not a misplaced expression of urban minimalism. The hotel has plenty of warmth and character – it's just not fussy. This suits the rugged surroundings rather well. Don't forget that at this altitude, the equivalent of the highest alpine village in France, temperatures plunge at night. Fireplaces may seem out of place during the 30°C daytime heat, but they become a welcome focus of cosy camaraderie in the evenings, when temperatures can drop as low as minus 2°C in the winter (June, July and August).

Proprietor Ricardo Quiros Nilo takes the hotel's oasis status seriously. Thus not only does La Aldea, rather unexpectedly, have a splendid pool, but Ricardo is also determined to keep the hotel small in order to encourage intimacy and interaction between fellow travellers. With the desert just beyond your window, La Aldea is the perfect base for your Atacama adventure.

---

address La Aldea, Aldea Solco, San Pedro de Atacama, Chile

telephone (56) 55 85 11 49 **fax** (56) 55 85 11 49

room rates from 46,000 Chilean Pesos

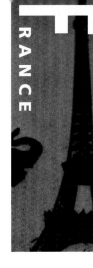

caron de beaumarchais

Inventor, clockmaker, musician, playwright, raconteur, aristocrat, political activist: Caron de Beaumarchais was one of the most colourful characters of eighteenth-century Paris. First and foremost he was one of Louis XV's favourite clockmakers, a position and title that provided him with an apartment in the Louvre and access to the king's inner circle. He was also the author of *The Marriage of Figaro*. Yet despite his links to the upper echelons of Bourbon power, he managed to escape the fate of most Parisian blue bloods thanks to his active sponsorship of the American Revolution. The hundreds of guns that he sold to America at no profit earned him the timely respect of France's Revolutionary Council.

Back then a character the likes of Beaumarchais would live in one area of Paris only – the Marais. In pre-revolutionary days, this was *the* scene for society dances and society duels. It was the heartland of elegant living and refined taste. But as Paris changed dramatically during France's tumultuous nineteenth century, the Marais was left behind. While the rest of France's capital became a showcase of broad, beaming boulevards and sumptuously conceived four- or five-storey Haussmann apartment buildings, the Marais

remained a medieval maze of narrow streets and cobbled lanes. Even the once crème de la crème Place de Vosges became shabby as the Marais became the poor area of Paris. Finally, under Nazi occupation, it even lost its community, when the large Jewish population either fled or was forcibly deported to the death camps.

History and chance had pickled the Marais. By the late twentieth century, its rediscovery was only a matter of time. In the 1980s, put off by the prices and the establishment attitude of the formerly rebellious Left Bank, artists, film makers, fashion designers, decorators and boutique owners started to move into the Marais. Within a few years they had made it Paris's answer to Greenwich Village, full of shops, restaurants, design establishments and – above all – life.

These days the Marais has become one of Paris's favourite neighbourhoods with locals and visitors alike. While Montparnasse has its artistic heritage, St-Germain its show-off chic, and the Quartier Latin its bohemian flavour, the Marais has some of the city's best contemporary shops, galleries and restaurants, including Mariage Frères, the extraordinary colonial-era tea emporium and dining room.

Despite the building's tiny scale, there is a small courtyard garden overlooked by all floors

Caron de Beaumarchais is decorated in the lighter Gustavian version of the Louis XVI style

Famous in his day as a royal clockmaker, Beaumarchais is remembered today as the author of *The Marriage of Figaro*

Inside and out, this small hotel in the most fashionable part of the city fulfils every Parisian fantasy

Portraits, mirrors, candelabras, chandeliers, statuary … the full lexicon of classic French design is here

An impressively decorative chandelier is suspended in the small but elegant lobby

The breakfast room – very atmospheric and typically French – is tucked away in the hotel's *souterrain*

Detail, detail, detail – that's what makes Caron de Beaumarchais so special (that and being in the middle of the Marais)

An oval oil painting and Louis XVI furniture contribute to the casual but chic ambience of the breakfast room

Mirror, mirror on the wall – who's trawled the Paris fleamarkets to find us all? M. Bigeard, the owner, I guess

A display window overlooking a corner of the lobby encourages the common misconception that this is a shop

Once each room had been completely renovated, all the old bits (such as ceiling beams) were put back

Some of the rooms have tiny balconies that are just big enough to seat two for breakfast

The portrait of Caron de Beaumarchais adorns everything from the hotel china to the letterhead

A real wood fire in the lobby awaits guests returning on chilly winter evenings

A still life of oriental vases adorns the otherwise all-white tiles of the bathrooms

With a harpsichord and an eighteenth-century card table in the lobby, this hotel is often mistaken for an *antiquaire*

The rooms are uncluttered, sober and practical: there are little cutouts in the bed niche for glasses, books or jewelry

caron de beaumarchais

Only in the Marais can you truly experience the Paris of the eighteenth century – the Paris of intrigue, mystery and charm, before Haussmann threw the whole place open.

Caron de Beaumarchais is the perfect name for this small hotel, and not only because he used to live next door. It exemplifies a certain refined approach to life. I had walked past its immaculate blue-painted timber facade many times, assuming it to be a chic decorator's showroom or perhaps an antique shop. The tiny lobby features a rare pianoforte from 1792, a black marble Louis XV fireplace, an antique card table and a handful of gilded wall sconces and antique mirrors. That's a lot of detail and a lot of antique packed into a tiny space, and it typifies the formula proprietor Alain Bigeard has followed throughout his nineteen-room hotel. The ceiling of every guest room features twisted and mangled exposed oak beams. The furniture is Louis XVI (the simple and more elegant Gustavian variety), and the fabrics are from the venerable Paris textile house Nobilis Fontan. The impression is authentically antique, just as we would hope to find in Paris, but there are also some very modern luxuries, including brand-new bathrooms. The entire building was dismantled leaving only the eighteenth-century facade standing. All the beautiful old parts – like the ceiling beams and wrought-iron balustrade – were saved and installed in a completely new building that has lifts and up-to-date plumbing, wiring and telecommunications, including satellite TV. The effect is old, but the convenience is new.

If Caron de Beaumarchais sounds like the perfect Parisian hotel experience, that's because it is. There's really only one problem – you won't get a room unless you book well in advance. Six weeks is recommended. Why is it so affordable? The proprietor would not be comfortable charging more, even though he could. In that sense he fits perfectly. He and his hotel are a throwback to a long-gone era of discreet refinement and elegant living.

address Hôtel Caron de Beaumarchais, 12 rue Vieille-du-Temple, 75004 Paris, France

telephone (33) 1 42 72 34 12   fax (33) 1 42 72 34 63

room rates from FF 790

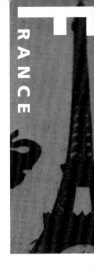
hôtel le corbusier

Marseilles used to be *the* place to avoid on a trip to the south of France. Just the way the locals drive (fast and rude) was enough to put you off. It was noisy and covered in graffiti, crime was out of control, the traffic was relentless, and anyone who had any sense had long ago moved to Aix. Marseilles was like New York in the seventies – it was mocked and feared, but from a safe distance; no one wanted to live there. But now, slowly, almost imperceptibly, the city is experiencing a renaissance. Fashion magazines have discovered the Vieux Port, the handsome marina in the well-preserved historic city centre with all its restaurants, brasseries and cafés. They have also discovered that this Provencal city, unlike Aix, Arles, and Avignon, has beaches. And unlike those of Cap d'Antibes, Cannes and Nice, they haven't yet been ruined.

So what has changed? Nothing really beyond perceptions – this is the same city seen in a different light. Film director Luc Besson realized for instance that the crime and the car culture balanced against the light, the weather and the scenery had great cinematic impact. As one of the Mediterranean's busiest ports, Marseilles still has a rough side, it's true, but that only adds to its character.

It's fair to say that Marseilles today is enjoying a level of tourism it hasn't known since the mid-twentieth century, when it was the port from which travellers departed for Africa. It's a stylish, streetwise city that boasts a long history. What it doesn't have, however, is a great choice of places to stay. There's a Novotel at the entrance of the old harbour, but however well located, a Novotel is still a Novotel – one step up from a hospital room in style and ambience, and then only just. There are some supposedly grand hotels at the other end of the marina, but I'm afraid they are 'grand' in a 1980s cocaine-dealer style: lots of beige, travertine and gold. You'd imagine Marseilles would have at least one hotel in line with its new hip profile. And in fact it does. The irony is that this hotel has been around since the mid-fifties, yet almost half a century later, few people know it's there. Extraordinary, particularly given that its designer happens to have been one of the twentieth century's greatest architects. Stranger still is that even among people who *are* aware of the building and its designer, including Le Corbusier aficionados (for this is one of his most famous projects), few realize that Unité d'Habitation has always contained a hotel.

Hôtel le Corbusier has changed neither in design nor in management for half a century. Admittedly, the rooms could do with a tiny facelift – there's nothing actually wrong with them, but at the same time they are not quite as pristine as one would expect from one of the acknowledged masters of modernism. This shortfall, however, is balanced by the quality of the building and, perhaps unexpectedly, by the quality of the location. Most people assume that Unité d'Habitation is in the grimmest part of town. After all, it started life as a housing project, didn't it? Well yes, but only because of a desperate shortage after World War II. In fact Le Corbusier's vertical city was built in one of the leafiest areas of Marseilles, and its roof has spectacular views of the bay and the headlands. Add to this the fact that it is surrounded by three hectares of park and it's easy to understand why all the apartments were snapped up by private buyers less than two years after the project was complete. Le Corbusier was decades ahead of his time, and not just in aesthetics, but in his conception of lifestyle. The gym on the roof for the adults combined with crèche and paddle pool for the kids predates today's 'mummy in the gym with a pram' culture by almost half a century. But that's the fun of staying in the Unité d'Habitation. The experience is both retro and futuristic, like living in a giant experimental project from the past.

Frank Lloyd Wright, Mies van der Rohe and Le Corbusier represent the very pinnacle of twentieth-century modernist architecture. Mies never designed a hotel; Wright did – the Imperial in Tokyo – but it burned down. That makes Le Corbusier's Unité d'Habitation unique. And not only do you get the bonus of a rehabilitated city to explore and empty beaches to play on, you also get to return to your residence in a Corbusier masterpiece smug in the knowledge that all those architecture students and Corb groupies haven't got a clue that they could actually stay here. If only they had studied the plans more thoroughly.

---

address Hôtel Le Corbusier, 280 boulevard Michelet – 3ème étage, 13008 Marseilles, France

telephone (33) 4 91 16 78 00   **fax** (33) 4 91 16 78 28

room rates from FF 225

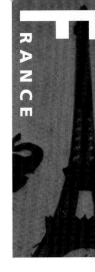

la manufacture

As in London and New York, a hotel room in Paris can be a problem, particularly if you're on a budget. It's difficult enough to find a place that's affordable; almost impossible to find one that's attractive *and* affordable; and completely unheard of to come across a hotel that's attractive, affordable, and well situated. That's why La Manufacture is such a great find. Situated on the edge of the Quartier Latin, it's only a hop, skip and a jump from the bars, restaurants, and jazz clubs of this atmospheric part of Paris.

La Manufacture is located just off Avenue des Gobelins, a name that first entered the French vocabulary when Louis XIV designated it as the new location of Les Manufactures Royales. Colbert, the king's chief minister, shifted all of Paris's weavers to this one location so they could create tapestries of the same dazzling magnitude as the Sun King's ego. To ensure the work would be up to the king's extraordinarily baroque standards, Colbert appointed the royal first painter, Charles Le Brun, to be in charge of creative direction. In Louis XIV's time the subject of these tapestries was predictable enough – they were limited to depictions of the Sun King in heroic and mythological poses. Gobelins tapestries quickly became world renowned for their quality. They are still made today, if not with quite the same craftsmanship. Not that you can walk in off the street and buy one, any more than you could under the Bourbons. These celebrated workshops still work exclusively on orders from the head of state. The tapestries are used to decorate French embassies and the presidential palace, or given as gifts to foreign governments. Needless to say, their subject matter has expanded in scope since the days of Louis XIV; even Picasso and Dali had designs turned into Gobelins tapestries.

Aside from the workshops, this historic neighbourhood has been home to bohemian writers and the odd student rebellion. Great French thinkers like Voltaire, Hugo, and Zola are buried in the nearby Pantheon and the Jardin des Plantes is virtually next door. These botanical gardens, established in 1626, are an excellent park and also home to a natural history museum and a zoo. To get a taste of the real Paris in this area, you just need to wander down the hill from the Pantheon and turn into the picturesque Rue Mouffetard. One of the oldest streets in Paris, dating back to Roman times, this is home to many small shops, open-air markets and affordable restaurants.

Breakfast is served in an imaginatively designed space that is vaguely reminiscent of a railway carriage

The lamps in the lobby were custom-made in Spain; the abstract paintings are by Parisian artist Alberto Cont

La Manufacture is in a beautifully detailed nineteenth-century, limestone Haussmann building

Oak floors, cotton rugs, cotton furniture – the lobby space is a combination of natural surfaces and elegant restraint

Chic, pas cher should be the motto for this surprising inner-city Parisian hotel

En suite pristine white-tiled bathrooms are standard: all plumbing was renewed in the renovation process

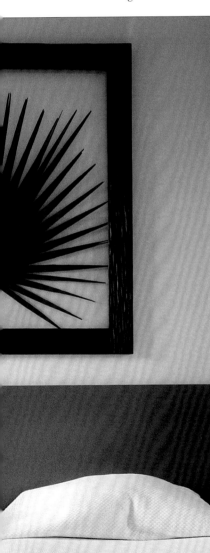

Paris is more fun when you don't feel like the chump tourist. What is so good about this area is that it is beautiful, historic and fascinating without ever being pretentious (as the Left Bank around Boulevard St-Germain can sometimes be). I for one can happily forgo the expensive cafés crammed with people, Prada boxes and Armani bags, as well as the so-called street buskers who turn up on cue every day at the same time to perform and extort. La Manufacture's neighbourhood on the other hand is personalized by the academic focus of the Sorbonne, the city's oldest university. Students have no interest in tourist traps – they want to blend in with the local scene, not unlike many of us visitors.

Although Paris is not a city where you should plan to spend a lot of time in your room, La Manufacture makes a pleasant environment to come back to. The exterior is pure nineteenth-century Haussmann: a grand five-storey limestone building with beautifully detailed wrought-iron balconies and relief carving to accentuate the classically proportioned doors and windows. Inside it's a different story – not quite minimalist but certainly contemporary and restrained. The pristine white walls are interrupted only by the vivid colour and geometry of paintings by local artist Alberto Cont. But long before they thought about the interior design, the three-woman consortium of proprietors subjected the building to a thorough renovation that involved knocking down walls and installing a lift, air conditioning and new plumbing throughout. The result is that the rooms benefit not only from crisp contemporary decoration but from contemporary conveniences, including brand new white-tiled bathrooms.

Oak floorboards, wicker chairs, cotton rugs, wooden furniture: these ingredients define a style that is both soft and natural, with none of the over-zealous patterning that Parisian hotels are prone to. What could possibly be better than an affordable, attractive, well-situated hotel in Paris? One that doesn't look affordable.

---

address   La Manufacture, 8 rue Philippe de Champagne, 75013 Paris, France

telephone (33) 1 45 35 45 25   fax (33) 1 45 35 45 40

room rates from FF 640

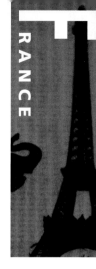

la maison rose

This pink, shuttered, ivy-covered mansion is a rare find. How many affordable hotels, after all, offer the cuisine of one of the most famous chefs in the world, as well as the thermal spa waters once patronized by the Empress Eugénie, wife of Napoleon III? Only one!

The chef I refer to is Michel Guérard, the man who invented nouvelle cuisine in the early seventies. Guérard is a culinary legend who has had his three Michelin stars for almost three decades and featured on the cover of *Time* magazine in 1976. His big-name contemporaries Alain Ducasse and Michel Troisgros started their careers in Guérard's kitchens here in the tiny but world-famous village of Eugénie-les-Bains.

Henry IV is rumoured to have sampled the waters here, and the Empress Eugénie made the 70-mile journey from Biarritz to enjoy the reputed beautifying qualities of this tiny village that came to be named after her. Fashionable France followed suit, and so did the French Ministry of Health, which still today prescribes cures at Eugénie les Bains for complaints such as obesity and rheumatism.

The 'treatment' that comes to mind these days when one thinks of Eugénie-les-Bains is 'being spoiled rotten'. That's because within the space of a couple of decades the Guérards have turned this sleepy rural spa into a hot hedonist destination.

The story of how this dynamic couple created an international name for their particular brand of 'French Bliss' is a bit of a fairy tale. It all began in the early seventies, when Michel Guérard had a tiny but excellent restaurant called Le Pot au Feu in a not too glamorous suburb of Paris. Christine Barthelemy had inherited a run-down hotel spa from her father, and, determined to revive it, she made the trip to Paris to seek Guérard's advice on her culinary approach. Guérard went to Eugénie with Christine and never left. As the locals like to say, 'the chef married the spa … and the spa owner'. They set about renovating the place and by 1974 they were able to open the first guest rooms. Christine Guérard was in charge of management and interior design; Michel, naturally enough, took care of the food.

It was tough in the beginning, but word began to spread of the innovations Guérard was up to in the kitchen. Repelled by the utter tastelessness of 'healthy food', he set about creating a cuisine that would delight both the palette and the bathroom scales. It was an unbeatable combination: his *cuisine minceur* was a big hit. His continuing experimentation and refinement soon won him three stars, Michelin's highest honour.

In the thirty-odd years since these humble beginnings, the Guérards have built a fully fledged empire. Michel Guérard now has his own wine label, his restaurant is a place of pilgrimage for serious foodies from all over the world, and in addition to the original hotel they now also operate a string of establishments: a former convent, the Couvant des Herbes, now a beautifully appointed retreat for eight guests; La Ferme aux Grives, an equally luxurious old farmhouse; another restaurant, also called La Ferme aux Grives, serving simpler fare at lower prices; and an elegantly converted manor house, La Maison Rose, which offers a less pricey accommodation alternative. Like all the other Guérard hotels, La Maison Rose is right in the middle of Eugénie-les-Bains, but its interiors are less grand. Given that this is a spa – a place of health rather than indulgence (in theory at least) – for many that feels quite

appropriate. The best thing about La Maison Rose is that despite the lower rates its guests have exactly the same access to the treatments and the food for which Eugénie is famous.

Set in an old farmhouse, the aesthetic of La Ferme Thermale is light years away from the clinical look we normally associate with spas. There are antique claw-footed baths, recovery rooms with Lutyens-inspired teak recliners, and a Chinese-style massage bed made entirely of (heated) white marble. There's even a bathing room entirely covered in white-tile mosaics whose plunge pool is filled to the brim with white kaolin clay. Guests in immaculate white waffle-cotton bathrobes relax between treatments by an enormous fire in the soaring 30-foot-high barn-like recovery room, sipping exotic oriental blends of juice and tea.

It's fair to say that the Guérards, with their devilishly seductive regime of design and cuisine, have reinvented the concept of a spa retreat. Sin while you slim? It's an irresistibly tempting package.

---

address La Maison Rose, Les Prés d'Eugénie, 40320 Eugénie-les-Bains, France

telephone (33) 5 58 05 06 07   **fax** (33) 5 58 51 10 10

room rates from FF 700

advokat

The Oktoberfest isn't the only thing Munich has going for it. This stylish city in Germany's Bavarian south can often feel more Italian than German. You may think Lederhosen, Weissbier, and Bratwurst when you think of Munich, but the reality is more like Zegna, Château Neuf du Pape, and cotolette alla Milanese.

This difference from the rest of Germany is understandable enough. Munich is much closer to Italy, Austria and Switzerland than to Hamburg, Frankfurt or Berlin. Over the centuries these Alpine neighbours have swapped borders and languages so often that you would expect some of this cultural exchange to remain in evidence. There's also of course an aesthetic benefit in being so close to the Alps. Munich is a city surrounded by majestic mountains, immense lakes and thick forests – a very different scenario to Germany's industrial, polluted north. Then there's the weather. Because it's further south the light and the climate are more agreeable. Admittedly Munich winters are cold, but at least it snows. Take all this into account, plus the city's wealth, and you can understand why Münchners have a reputation for being happy, hospitable people.

Munich is also the media capital of Germany. Film, television and radio are largely based here, as are industrial giants like BMW (their offices, not the factories). Like many sophisticated cities, it has used its wealth for beautification and for investment in museums and galleries. In the process, Munich has gained a reputation for the avant-garde. It is not perhaps as progressive as Berlin, but it has fostered homegrown talent like Ingo Maurer, one of the world's leading lighting designers, or Otto Frei, the architect who stunned the world in 1972 with his giant lightweight tent-like structures designed for the Munich Olympics.

Cultural credibility, however, usually goes hand in hand with an increased cost of living, and this Bavarian capital is no exception. Munich is a notoriously expensive town and until recently, unless you could afford to stay at the Rafael or the Vier Jahreszeiten, your prospects for a memorable and enjoyable hotel experience were bleak. That all changed when the Advokat came on the scene. This sixties office building (previously home to the Pfanni food group) was transformed by Kevin Voigt and Thomas Masermall into a stylish hotel that has rapidly become a magnet to a young fashion- and design-conscious clientele.

advokat

Voigt, who trained at Hamburg's Four Seasons, is a hotel professional. It is his attention to detail and understanding of service that makes this small, hip hotel more than just a groovy collection of half-empty white boxes. The little touches are what make it a place you'd come back to – touches like the complimentary self-service bar in the lobby and the fresh fruit and coffee served on the roof terrace in summer. Even mainstream magazines such as *Travel & Leisure* have commented favourably on the Advokat breakfast. It may be a buffet affair but nobody's complaining when the choice includes kiwis, strawberries, raspberries, blackberries, figs, meats, cheeses, pastries and croissants – and that's just a shortlist.

So breakfast is worth coming down for – but what are the rooms like? One critic summed the design up as 'Philippe Starck on a shopping binge at Ikea.' He was right: there's a twist to the design (typical Starck) even if it didn't cost that much money (typical Ikea). A red apple, for example, is left in a carefully

created dent in the pillows, and an unassuming stainless steel frame holds a black and white postcard that changes on a regular basis.

None of this is earth-shatteringly original but neither is it typical hotel fare. The trick is not to scrutinize under a microscope but to imagine what the hotel would be like without these careful touches. Another journalist put it well by describing the hotel and its rooms as 'soberly opulent' – a pretty accurate oxymoron.

The only thing I couldn't figure out was the name. Why Advokat, meaning the lawyer? They will tell you it refers to the functional aesthetic by which this place has been renovated. Clear as mud, then. And why is Voigt and Masermall's other Munich hotel called the Admiral? Because, I am told, it's done in a more classical style to appeal to lawyers and businessmen. So here's a final question. If the Lawyer is designed for designers and the Admiral is designed for lawyers, who would they target with a hotel called the Surgeon?

address Advokat, Baaderstrasse 1, 80469 Munich, Germany
telephone (49) 89 21 63 10 **fax** (49) 89 21 63 190
room rates from DM 290

hotel gastwerk

Five thousand tons of coal are not exactly conventional credentials for a hotel site. Yet that's exactly what Hamburg's Hotel Gastwerk used to accommodate before it swapped coal for paying guests. It takes a gigantic leap of imagination to stand in front of an eighty-six-thousand-square-foot dilapidated power plant – a very *schmutzig* one at that, oozing coal dust out of every pore – and envisage its potential as a hotel. And it takes an even greater leap of faith to commence the gargantuan task of turning it into just that.

A typical property developer would covet such a structure only for the land it is standing on. First step would be to knock the whole thing down and start from scratch. Who would bother to keep on a dysfunctional old industrial giant, even given the sheer space that it encompasses? How many people truly appreciate the abstract aesthetics of huge pressed-metal funnels, rusty cogs and other massive oxidized equipment? Well, a lot more than we could possibly have imagined half a century ago. London's Tate Modern is another enormous former power station, originally designed by Giles Gilbert Scott and recently converted by the hot architectural duo of Herzog and de Meuron, and it has proved

incredibly successful. With no disrespect to the art within, it's the building that people really come to experience. Similarly, half way around the globe, another brick Godzilla was converted into Sydney's hugely popular Powerhouse Museum. In Paris, the Gare d'Orsay was an industrial leftover that in spite of its fine external detailing was in danger of a confrontation with the demolition ball. Instead Italian architect Gae Aulenti's creative reinvention of this railway yard has made the Musée d'Orsay one of the most visited landmarks in a city that's not exactly short of things to see. The age of industry, it seems, has more appeal and charisma than anyone might have imagined a few decades ago.

With such recent precedents on their side, the new proprietors set out to be the first to turn a relic from the industrial age into a place to sleep. The brief they came up with for designers Regine Schwethelm and Sybille von Heyden was very straightforward. The hotel had to house one hundred rooms plus all the facilities that make for a happy guest: a good restaurant, a funky bar and a gym (or a 'well-being area', as they like to refer to it in Germany). All this was built, and in each respect with great success. But the Gastwerk

was also designed to cater to a different breed of hotel guest – the day guest. Local Hamburgers can meet in style in the lofty spaces of the machine hall. The logic behind this provision is perfectly lucid. How, the proprietors argue, can people possibly be expected to be creative, inventive and inspired when they are cooped up in the dismal cramped spaces of their everyday lives? When they come to Gastwerk they are in an environment utterly different from where they normally work, wherever that may be. Thus part of the massive space of the former machine hall was given over to some twenty conference rooms. When the conference guests emerge for a break, they are catered for in the seven-storey space of the machine hall. In one fell swoop Hotel Gastwerk has very successfully set itself up to cater to both the local population and out-of-towners. It's a clever concept.

But as for out-of-towners, what is it like to stay here? The word that comes to mind is spacious – cavernously spacious. The rooms are large, the restaurant is big, the bar is huge, and the atrium is vast. So often less expensive also means less spacious, but this place is a space feast. They could easily have squeezed many more guest rooms into the complex, but you will be glad they didn't. The management here very clearly understand what makes us out-of-towners tick.

The other advantage of Hotel Gastwerk is that they have managed to retain an industrial edge throughout, even in the bedrooms. Rugged, unrendered, unpainted brick walls go well with the slick but simple MDF furniture and the brand new white-tiled bathrooms. Bedspreads decorated with Chinese script and sliding vertical panels complete the picture. The rooms manage to be comfortable living spaces at the same time as retaining the traces of their industrial past.

I guess it took the dawning of the electronic age to make the machine age a romantic proposition.

---

address Hotel Gastwerk, Forum Altes Gastwerk, Daimlerstrasse 67, 22761 Hamburg, Germany

telephone (49) 40 890 62 445   **fax** (49) 40 890 62 20

room rates from DM 195

hotel pelirocco

Rave all night, sleep all day. For many visitors to Brighton that's the attraction. Clubbing in Brighton is an event. It's theatrical, inventive, and nothing if not outrageous. Performance artists like Leigh Bowery made their name with the publicity generated by their outfits. Countless documentaries have been made, all concerned – from all different angles – with the spectacle of Brighton clubbing.

Brighton is almost the Ibiza of the north, minus the weather of course, but with the distinct advantage of being a train- rather than a plane-journey from London. Travelling to Brighton is not a new phenomenon. Mods on scooters with an excess of rearview mirrors and rockers with their slicked-back hair used to migrate in huge convoys. Brighton was the inspiration behind The Who's movie (and soundtrack) Quadrophenia, and the town has always featured large in the British music scene. Most recently Skint Records, a local label, has had huge international success with recording artist Fatboy Slim. With such an historic and contemporary music and clubbing scene, it's really rather surprising that this old seaside town until recently had no hotel that catered to its hipper clientele. It has plenty of cheap chintzy hotels, for sure, and a handful

of expensive chintzy hotels, but none that even remotely reflect the town's style status. No doubt many music-minded nocturnal tourists had lamented this, but one couple decided to do something about it. Mick Robinson and Jane Slater were reasonably representative London–Brighton clubbers: he was in the fashion business and had done the odd stint as a club DJ (under the name Pelirocco), while she worked in PR in London. They had done both the cheap and the not-so-cheap chintz too many times, and it was during an early morning conversation full of ideas and solutions that the 'what if' and 'we should' turned into 'we will'.

So the hard work began. The banks weren't interested, despite an obvious gap in the market, so in the end they established a syndicate comprised mainly of friends to fund the purchase of a perfect venue in Regency Square, one of the most attractive and intact parts of Regency Brighton, directly opposite the esplanade and the famous Brighton pier (which by the way is rumoured to be in for an extensive renovation by Terence Conran and Oliver Peyton). The double-fronted listed Georgian property was designated for eighteen guest rooms, a bar, a breakfast area and a conference room.

Once past the not insignificant paperwork hurdle – business plans, profit projection, construction costs, planning permission and so on – the focus turned to the rooms and what they should look like. From the very beginning, Mick and Jane knew they wanted each one to be different – completely different. That in itself is not an original idea in the current hip hotel world, but their approach was. The rooms vary from an orange chamber covered top to bottom in black polka dots, to Modrophenia, a purple room complete with mod scooter. Unlike the Madonna Inn in California, which specializes in the tasteless and tacky, the themes at Pelirocco are not just the product of whimsy. They pay tribute to artists such as Yayoi Kusama (the orange polka dot room), and Leigh Bowery, whose room, decorated by his widow, is papered with his press clippings. Skint Records decorated a room, as did Jamie Reid, the innovative graphic talent behind the Sex Pistols in the eighties. What at first glance may seem completely off the wall in fact reflects an eclectic set of inspirations: exhibitions they have been to, music labels they admire and cult books all play a role. A further twist is the introduction of sponsors. That's how the hotel ended up with a PlayStation bar and a console in every room, a Nokia conference room and an Absolut Love room. A Japanese clubland character, complete with shades, fag and orange hair, is the Absolut pin-up boy of the breakfast menu. But this branding is never over the top or out of place. The sponsors were chosen as carefully as the room themes, and it shows.

And in case you are wondering, all this anti-convention does not interfere with the hotel experience. The bottom line is that the Hotel Pelirocco delivers spacious rooms, modern bathrooms and full mod cons (internet plug-in points, satellite TV, air conditioning). And most importantly for those allergic to a standard 11 o'clock checkout, the hotel has a 2 pm checkout for an extra £10. So you really can rave all night, sleep all day.

address Hotel Pelirocco, 10 Regency Square, Brighton BN1 2FG, Great Britain
telephone (44) 1273 327 055 **fax** (44) 1273 733 845
room rates from £45 (including breakfast)

the big sleep

It all started with a chocolate bar – not the kind you eat, but a café that specializes in hot chocolate in the way that the Seattle Coffee Company or the Coffee Republic specialize in coffee. This was the dream of Cosmo Fry – entrepreneur, budding industrialist and great great grandson of the inventor of Fry's chocolate bar – and Lulu Anderson, fashion editor for the Daily Telegraph. Together they went in search of a venue for their new bar. The very first building they saw was a perfectly located site in Bristol. The only trouble was that the tenant had to take the whole building, and neither Cosmo nor Lulu had anticipated such a commitment. What would they do with the space? The idea of opening a hotel in conjunction with their chocolate bar occurred to them, but it seemed an unfeasibly huge project, and they decided not to put in an offer. Gradually, however, the hotel idea took hold; then it became a driving passion; and finally the chocolate bar fell out of the equation altogether, never to make it into the final plans.

The building they settled on was a gem, a former office block in the heart of Cardiff that had already been converted – badly – into a hotel. The orange and purple colour scheme had to go, but the all-white bathrooms, almost all with windows, could stay. The idea was to create a modern hotel for travellers on a budget: bright, pared-down and hip – design without the design-label price tag. The constraints were formidable. The renovation budget was paltry, and their only unrestricted resources were imagination and Formica … yes, Formica. For while most of his contemporaries had ended up with buttoned-down jobs in the City, Cosmo followed his inventor-entrepreneur father's example and purchased a run-down Formica business in 1981. Slowly, diligently, he re-established Formica as a brand and a stylish surfacing option in the UK. The hotel in Cardiff presented him with a golden opportunity to experiment with its possibilities.

Formica, as Cosmo Fry explains (and he loves talking about the stuff), has great creative and aesthetic potential. Different colours can be combined to create amazing 3-D effects. Bedheads and built-in bedside tables at the Big Sleep have white horizontal surfaces contrasted with vertical stripes of baby blue, lilac, or Burberry-style tartan. The idea of a bedroom furnished largely in Formica would normally make me think Hospital, but here it is used in a highly original way that will doubtless rekindle interest in this classic modern material.

Even the picture frames displaying giant Mario Testino photos from a recent Burberry campaign were constructed in black formica with internal detailing in white.

For those who still fear that this may be a bit hard and clinical, there is a foil to the Formica in the form of fleece and fur. Lulu Anderson discovered – much to her surprise – that some of the most affordable furnishing options were also the most tactile. Fleece fabric (the stuff of toddlers' playsuits) and fake fur (the kind used for teddy bears) were not only inexpensive, but soft, cuddly and warm, making them the perfect 'touch-me-feel-me' contrast to the angular geometrics of the Formica. They are also very practical: the weight and thickness of the cloth make it a very effective barrier against light and noise. When you draw the curtains before the wall-to-wall glass, you're cocooned in a surround-sound environment of fluffy fleece. Finally, Cosmo and Lulu chose furniture to round out the effect: a polypropylene Robin Day chair, for

example, is used like a giant piece of costume jewelry. The most convincing design feature of the Big Sleep, however, is the light. The building, originally the Cardiff headquarters of British Gas, is a glass tower whose interior is filled with daylight – the perfect complement to the crisply creative design.

Fleece, fur, formica, furniture – and a film star as a partner in the hotel. The invitations to the opening of the Big Sleep were surreal. At the time that *Being John Malkovich* was on general release across Britain, a pale blue card invited guests to breakfast in bed with John Malkovich. What kind of trick was this? Surely they didn't mean *the* John Malkovich? But the promotion was unequivocal: enter the contest sponsored by a local radio station and you could be one of the lucky few to have breakfast in bed with John Malkovich. The opening day arrived. The press – understandably sceptical – turned up, as did the contest winners, to find John Malkovich in his jimjams in bed in the lobby of the Big Sleep hotel.

---

address The Big Sleep, Bute Terrace, Cardiff CF10 2FE, Great Britain

telephone (44) 2920 63 63 63   **fax** (44) 2920 63 63 64

room rates from £45 (including breakfast)

the penzance arts club

Penzance is known as the end of England. From here you can go no further south and no further west. The next piece of land is the USA. Tucked into the westernmost corner of Cornwall, an area that is already remote from the rest of England, Penzance is one of the most perfect escape destinations in the UK. Apart from being romantically remote, it sports a very photogenic coastline, a wild and rugged landscape steeped in Celtic myth and legend, and a picturesque town architecture rich in elegant Georgian heritage as well as charming fishermen's cottages.

Penzance is also second only to London in its resident population of working artists. Just as Jackson Pollock found his inspiration in the charm and character of the hamlets of the Hamptons, artists such as Ben Nicholson and Barbara Hepworth as well as authors like D.H. Lawrence made this area famous. Even Mondrian spent time in Penzance and was a fan of the St Ives School, the embodiment of all that was modern, avant-garde and bohemian in mid-twentieth-century England. The Tate Gallery in nearby St Ives is devoted to this artistic heritage.

These days, surfers, sculptors, painters, fishermen, farmers and more than a handful of urban refugees continue to make Penzance the most bohemian place in England – and thus the perfect location for textile designer Belinda Rushworth-Lund's Arts Club. Situated at the lower end of picturesque and historic Chapel Street in a handsome 1781 Grade II listed Georgian townhouse that was once the Portuguese embassy (back when Penzance was a major sea port), the club currently claims three hundred members, including some of England's most accomplished painters. The lounge bar (in the former state rooms of the embassy) is their local, and the convivial club atmosphere is a signature of the place.

Thankfully, one does not need to be a member to stay here. With fine views of the beaches and the much-painted St Michael's Mount, the Penzance Arts Club has all that you might want from a hotel: generous rooms, great view, and masses of character. In step with the name and the *simpatico* feel of the place, the hotel also organizes fine arts courses. On the night I arrived there, a still-life drawing class was under way. Behind a veil of thick velvet curtains eight students were rendering their interpretations of a model posed by the fireplace. Nothing could illustrate more vividly the credentials and the atmosphere.

The Beach, the Penzance Arts Club's basement restaurant in surfer shades, has several tons of sand on the floor

The former entrance hall is now used as a gallery where fortnightly exhibitions are held

As suits such an eccentric place, each guest room is different. The peach room has a fireplace and old floorboards

The building, at one time the Portuguese embassy, is a stately Georgian mansion overlooking the sea

The blue room, the largest upstairs guest room, is colourful, cluttered and eclectic in a grand but charming way

More 'piled up' than 'put together', the style of this quirky Cornwall hotel is shabby bohemian chic

In every respect the place is true to its name. The original formal entrance – a handsome hallway illuminated by a Georgian fanlight – serves as a gallery space for fortnightly exhibitions, and elsewhere throughout the hotel the walls and spaces are dense with paintings, drawings, collages and sculptures by member artists. Combined with a scattering of antiques, refectory chairs, big easy velvet-covered sofas, driftwood candlesticks, beaten-up floorboards and loose rugs, plus the odd chandelier, the look and the ambience have been variously described as 'Bloomsbury by the sea' or 'Chelsea with a view'.

A real surprise awaits the guest ready to sample the hotel's inventively tasty food. Located in what were the Portuguese embassy's kitchens, the Beach Restaurant provides a further bohemian twist with its floor covered in half a foot of fine pale beach sand. The odd surfboard leaning casually against the walls and a colour scheme of acid blues, yellows and greens complete the picture: it's the ultimate beach bum's bomb shelter. But claustrophobes fear not – double doors opening out onto the garden prevent the space from feeling too subterranean.

Upstairs, the guest rooms are very spacious, just as one would expect of a Georgian house, and – more surprising – very colourful. There's a blue room, a yellow room, a peach room and of course a white room. Most have a view of the ocean and the beaches. In summer, yoga classes are held in the walled gardens. Even the dark blue men's room has a view over the white scallop of Penzance's famous shoreline. But it is in the former stable room of the ground floor, painted in a warm shade of burnt ochre, that the personality of this bohemian bolt hole finds its truest expression. With a fire burning cosily at either end of the room and the evening's personalities ensconced in their favourite wicker chairs or at the old oak table by the window, the atmosphere will make you think seriously about returning for a week of landscape painting or life-drawing.

address The Penzance Arts Club, Chapel House, Chapel Street, Penzance, Cornwall TR18 4AQ, Great Britain

telephone (44) 1736 363 761 **fax** (44) 1736 363 761

room rates from £30 (including breakfast)

hotel bratsera

Litmos, Naxos, Patmos, Paros, Mykonos, Zakinthos, Lesbos…the sheer number of Greek islands presents a bewildering choice. With so many options, which do you choose, and why?

One of the smallest stands out. Hydra is unlike all other Greek islands – and not just because it doesn't end in '-os'. It hasn't been marred by mass tourism, and it's one of very few islands that doesn't allow vehicles of any kind – cars, motorcycles, scooters, mopeds, even bicycles. Horses, mules, donkeys and feet are the only available means of transport. This means that Hydra has avoided that most irritating plague of the Mediterranean – teenagers and tourists on whining, two-stroke-engined two-wheelers circling the town like Sioux Indians on the warpath until the early hours of the morning.

The only motors you will hear on Hydra are the burbling engines of the hydrofoil or the high-speed catamaran ferry that pulls in briefly to drop off and pick up passengers to the mainland. Hydra is a perfectly charming cluster of traditional houses hugging an old horseshoe-shaped harbour with the odd windmill and some remote monasteries in the barren hills beyond. It has no high-rise buildings, no hideous concrete bunkers and no huge hotel.

But wait – it gets better. Hotel Bratsera, like Hydra itself, is one-of-a-kind. Architecturally, I admit I was sceptical. What, I thought, could possibly be done with a whitewashed house except something simple and predictable? Blue doors, thatched wooden chairs, that sort of thing. I was certainly not prepared for a building that won a Europa Nostra diploma in 1996 for outstanding restoration. Until the mid-eighties, Bratsera was a factory – a sponge factory. Originally established by Nickolaos Verneniotis in 1860, this was where his family's eighteen-odd boats and their divers would return with sea sponges plucked from the bottom of the Mediterranean. In the factory the sponges were cleaned, bleached, trimmed into neat shapes and then placed in a massive press to compact them ready for shipping.

Customers were as far-flung as the Swedish post office, which used sponge for wetting stamps, and French porcelain manufacturers, who used it for protective packaging – plus of course the trade in bath sponges. But a once-thriving business was transformed in the years after the Second World War by the availability of cheap plastic sponges. At the same time, the countries bordering the Med started to police their national waters more vigorously.

Greek sponge divers found themselves no longer welcome in the waters of Lebanon, Syria, Turkey and Cypress.

The current proprietor of the Bratsera hotel, Christine Davros, grew up surrounded by sponges. The factory was her family's business, and up until 1986 she was in charge of exports. But as the years went by, it was ever more difficult to stay afloat, and it was she who made the decision to convert from sponges to hospitality. The factory, a stone's throw from the picturesque harbour, was the perfect venue for a highly individual hotel. It was spacious enough to house a bar, restaurant, courtyard swimming pool, gallery, and hall with capacity for over one hundred; and it provided the raw ingredients and the inspiration for a highly inventive design approach.

Architect Dimitris Papaharalambous successfully integrated the signature features of the sponge factory into a highly effective design scheme. The doors of the twenty-three guest rooms, for example, were constructed from recycled packing crates, with their stencilled destinations still legible. The sponge press and other old factory equipment adorns the public areas as carefully placed sculpture. Vintage black and white photos from the heyday of the sponge factory decorate the guest rooms. But the industrial theme goes beyond cleverly conceived decoration. It is present in the very construction materials: in the window frames of robust angle steel, in the staircase composed of two massive steel girders, in the rough and rugged stone walls, and in floors of unfinished broad pine planking. Together with the polished-granite ground floor, it all combines to create a style and ambience that is not only thoroughly individual but entirely unexpected for a hotel in such an idyllic little village.

The most telling Hydra statistic is the fact that more than forty Athens-based architects have houses here: Greece's cultural and aesthetic elite have chosen Hydra as their weekend getaway and summer retreat. It's no accident that the island remains so unspoiled.

address   Hotel Bratsera, Hydra 180 40, Greece

telephone   (30) 2 98 53 971   fax   (30) 2 98 53 626

room rates   from 33,000 Drachma (including breakfast)

les terrasses

Ibiza – catch the wrong television programme and the very word will fill you with dread. If, specifically, you caught any part of the documentary 'Ibiza Uncovered', then you might have concluded that this is the last place any sane person would want to go to. Raving, sunburned clubbers by the charter-planeload are hardly a come-hither siren call for those seeking the natural beauty and simple way of life for which this Balearic island was once famed.

But the reality is that Ibiza still has both – it has the notorious club scene, with thousands of buckskin-clad clubbers who come to the island to sun, eat, drink, dance, sun, eat, drink, drink, dance, drink and sleep. And it also has the idyllic coves, white-sand beaches, azure blue water, whitewashed fincas and terracotta-tiled roofs that made Ibiza famous in the first place. The clubland tourism is located mainly in and around the town of Sant Miguel. Beyond that, Ibiza still has plenty of destinations that make a largely rural impression. One such place, hidden away on a hillside en route to Santa Eulàlia, is Les Terrasses. Like most hotels with lots of character and lots of charm, it was never meant to be a hotel. Françoise Pialoux first came to Ibiza when it was the hippy

place-to-be in the sixties and early seventies, and never left. The hotel's original little whitewashed house was her own hideaway, and she built another just above it to accommodate the friends who always seemed to be dropping in. Another house followed and then another, and then a pool, and on it went. Françoise couldn't stop building. First the property became a guest house, and in the shortest time a hotel – a very popular hotel.

Almost by accident, Les Terrasses has become the ideal finca for those who don't have their own. It's a collection of typical Ibizenco dwellings – whitewashed (of course) and pure and simple in design – the kind that seem to attract everyone from famous musicians to retired architects. Belgian architect Philippe Rothier, a specialist in the traditional buildings of Ibiza, likes to call them *les palais paysans* – peasant palaces. Historically, their every measurement was based on the human form. But if that's the appeal, it is largely subliminal. Closer to the truth is the fact that on vacation we all want to escape day-to-day responsibilities, especially one as mundane as maintenance. Being so simple and well-suited to the climate, fincas are in this respect particularly undemanding.

Even for the non-party crowd, Ibiza – far more than Formentera or Mallorca or Menorca – is an outdoor island. There are no palaces or grand estates or old family piles outside Ibiza town. Despite the tourism, it's still an island of great rural beauty. Perhaps most distinctive are the myriad of little coves called *calas*, nestled among the hills and cliffs that lead down to the water on all sides of the island. Inland from the coast the island still has much of the pine forest that prompted the ancient Greeks to refer to this and Formentera as the Pityusae or pine islands. And although tourism is big business, the island still sustains a rural economy. Off the beaten track, small farms and market gardens grow carab, corn, grapes, figs, almonds, pears, and even hemp and flax.

The flipside of holidaying on Ibiza of course is that when you are tired of swimming in crystal clear *calas*, and making excursions to the local farmer to buy olives, you can always head out to Ibiza Town for some nightlife. The marina district is filled with cafés and bars, or you can dine in a small exclusive restaurant in D'Alt Vila or upper town, a recently restored and very fine example of sixteenth-century Spanish military architecture complete with a warren of narrow medieval streets and a huge gothic cathedral. Afterwards, there are always the clubs.

And what of Ibiza's reputation as the Mediterranean's most frenetic party island? It's true that on some early summer mornings you can make out the faint thump of a mighty bass beat, but, like the early explorers, if you don't trust the noise of a distant tribe, don't venture any closer. Historically speaking, this more demonstrative side to Ibiza's split personality is really nothing new. The locals certainly aren't too concerned – for them it's simply a matter of history repeating itself. The Romans used to call Ibiza by the Greek name Illa Gymnasia because of the inhabitants' apparent fondness for running around without any clothes. *Plus ça change.*

---

address Les Terrasses, Can Vich, Carretera de Santa Eulàlia km 1, Apdo 1235, Ibiza, Spain

telephone (34) 971 332 643   fax (34) 971 338 978

room rates from 15,500 Pesetas (including breakfast)

nilaya hermitage

Nilaya, roughly translated, means 'blue heaven' in Sanskrit. It's an appropriate name. Perched on top of a jungle peak in tropical Goa, the Nilaya Hermitage is an exquisite blue sanctuary with spectacular views of swaying palms and the Arabian Sea below. It architectural signature is incredibly eclectic: there are Indian, Mexican, Balinese, New Age and organic influences, as well as borrowings from Gaudi and the styles of colonial Goa. And that's just the architecture: the interior detailing is an even more exotic mix of cosy French, minimal Mexican, and streamlined Rajasthani.

This ethno-eclecticism makes perfect sense when you consider the lives of its proprietors, Claudia Derain and Hari Ajwani. Hari was born in India, educated in Germany, and worked in Europe as an engineer before returning to his native Goa. Claudia, the creative engine of the project, is even more international: with a German mother and a French diplomat father, she has lived in more countries than most people visit in a lifetime.

But if part of Nilaya's charm owes to its creators being citizens of the world, it is also due to the spontaneity of the project. Claudia and Hari never intended to build a portion of paradise from scratch. They already had a colonial house in Goa, and by all accounts it was a very beautiful one: it had the high ceilings, wooden floors, and all the style of Goa's four centuries of Portuguese heritage. They operated it as a successful upmarket *maison d'hôte*. There was only one snag. Although they had completely renovated the place, they didn't legally own it. The proprietor had promised to sell it to them (eventually), but no more than that. Then an old Portuguese law cropped up prohibiting the sale of a family property without written agreement from every single living member of the family. When an aunt in Mumbai refused point blank, that was that.

Feeling devastated, frustrated, and decidedly ripped off, they set out to find somewhere new. The first and most logical place to look was the coast, but the right property failed to turn up. In any case, given the rate tourism was developing in Goa, they feared being rapidly swallowed up by hideous development. Then a substantial plot on a hilltop in the hinterland became available. At first they both dismissed it outright – what would they do there? It would be too difficult to get to, too hot, and it was not exactly walking distance from the beaches, Goa's key attraction.

The gold star with southern Indian
features is a perfect symbol for Nilaya
Hermitage

Pure simplicity and pure colour, with
the odd colonial piece as a reminder of
Goa's four centuries of Portuguese rule

Nilaya's swimming pool covered entirely
in broken-tile mosaic is vast and deep,
so the water doesn't get too warm

Eating on and under the stars: dinner is served on a raised outdoor platform with views over palms and the shore

Blue is proprietor and designer Claudia Derain's favourite colour, and metallic sheen her favourite highlight

The homage to Gaudi is continued in the bathrooms. This one incorporates mirrors in its broken-tile design

Even so, Hari suggested hiring a team with machetes to chop their way to the top and at least peek at what was on offer. There they discovered not just a vista of swaying palms and distant beaches, but also a cool breeze wafting up the mountain – much cooler than by the sea. Their decision was swift. With no plan clearer than a determination to create another exceptional guest house, they got started. The work took three years in all. First they had to build access roads, and then clear the site – this was, after all, a patch of jungle. When they finally started building there was still no masterplan. As Claudia tells it, things evolved on a daily basis – which explains why Nilaya gives the impression of having been nurtured, not manufactured…grown, not designed.

With the exception of the odd gold dome and the mosaic-tiled swimming pool, the exterior is rugged rather than pretty, its porous brown volcanic stone blending perfectly with the verdant natural setting. It sets up a dramatic contrast with the interior, where all is blue: light blue terrazzo; washed blue walls accented by silver and gold paint; aquamarine surfaces contrasted by traditional pots in copper and gold. The colours, the Rajasthani antiques, the undulating surfaces and carefully arranged objects create a multi-ethnic melange. So distinctive is Claudia and Hari's approach that guests' constant inquiries of 'where did you get this' and 'where did you get that' eventually led to a shop. No half-measures for these two, though. In a step that brought them full circle, they acquired a beautiful dilapidated colonial building by the coast and created not just a shop but an entire complex dedicated to the Nilaya look and the Nilaya lifestyle. This is no run-of-the-mill showroom. It's a spectacular house, complete with bedrooms, living rooms, dining rooms, etc. The only difference is that everything in these immaculate spaces is always for sale and always changing. Here, as at Nilaya, you feel at once relaxed and inspired, happy to be immersed in a style the likes of which you will not have experienced before.

address Nilaya Hermitage, Arpora Bhatti, Goa 403518, India

telephone (91) 832 276 793/794 **fax** (91) 832 276 792

room rates from US$130 (including breakfast and transfers)

samode haveli

As India changes at extraordinary speed, cultural authenticity is fast becoming one of the country's most sought-after commodities. Let's face it – none of us travels to India in order to drive Japanese cars, eat at McDonald's or drink Coca Cola. The fact that India now has all of these, when only a decade ago it had none, is testament to the speed and scale of change. But with this unrelenting drive towards modernity has come an ironic turnaround for tourism. Whereas discerning visitors once searched for an oasis of Western comfort, now they seek the real India.

But what is the real India? The answer to that is as manifold as India itself. For many visitors, however, especially first-time visitors, the real India is Rajasthan. This is the India of maharajas and their intricate palaces, of men with bright turbans and women with equally vivid saris – bolts of gem-like colour in a land of heat and dust. Rajasthan is the India made famous by E.M. Forster's *A Passage to India*. And despite progress the good news is that the beauty and the spectacle that inspired books and films is still there to see and experience.

The declaration of independence in 1947 brought an abrupt end to the privileges and the income of India's famous princes. The maharajas no longer enjoyed the tax revenues that the British had allowed them to raise. Although they still had their palaces and properties, in most cases they had no way of maintaining them. Many highnesses had no choice but to become hoteliers. Of the 800-odd palaces that still stand in Rajasthan today, about 150 have been converted to hotels, some with more success than others. Many former maharajas went to great lengths to ensure the comfort of their Western guests – with the result that numerous palaces have been effectively ruined. The famous palace that stands majestically in the middle of Udaipur Lake, for instance, still looks splendid from the outside, but the interior is a cross between a Middle Eastern Hilton and a Bollywood filmset. Many more have suffered the same fate.

Fortunately, some of the Rajput aristocracy realized before it was too late that the best way to convert their former homes into successful hotels was to change nothing. Who cares about minibars, plastic hair dryers and cable TV when you can spend the night in a room once reserved for the conduct of a maharaja's amorous liaisons? What we want above all else is fantasy, and a maharaja's palace, preferably an *unconverted* one, fits the bill perfectly.

In the maharaja's mirrored playroom, dabs of coloured light reflect on the seemingly endless reflective surfaces

Mughal architecture was a distinctive blend of the invading Muslim culture and the indigenous Hindu one

This frescoed alcove in the dining room of the Samode Haveli is an exquisite example of local decorative tradition

The substantial gardens to the rear of this city palace are often used for lunches and parties

Complex geometric patterns carved into stone filter the daylight entering one of the guest rooms

Pale floors and walls with bold coloured outlines are typical of the decor of a Rajasthani palace bedroom suite

Given that there are so many palaces in Rajasthan, where does one start? The simple answer is in Jaipur – or, more accurately, within the old city walls of the famed pink city. Jaipur is the heart of Rajasthan, and for many centuries it was the seat of the state's ruling dynasty. Granted, the city has been modernized quite considerably, but from within the old walls, it's still possible to glimpse the magic and romance of days gone by – especially if you are staying at the Samode Haveli. Until quite recently, this was the townhouse of the Singhji family of Samode. The family's title came from the principality and palace of Samode, and dates back more than four centuries to the seventeenth-century prince Prithviraj Singhji of Amber. Samode is a beautiful, remote and mountainous stretch of Rajasthan, and the Samode palace is as impressive as its surroundings. But in more recent times, the family lived in their Jaipur *haveli*, using the palace in Samode mainly for holidays and special events. Eventually, in 1985, they made the inevitable decision to convert it to a hotel. Meanwhile, the family continued to occupy their city residence within the walls of old Jaipur. But even this in time proved too cumbersome to maintain – *haveli* may literally mean townhouse, but city palace is a far better description. Thus in 1994 they decided to convert it too into a hotel. By that time, visitors' desire for authenticity was an unmistakable trend, and thus the original rooms were hardly touched, with the exception, where necessary, of updating the electrics, plumbing and telecommunications.

The result is a style that may be summed up as 'maharaja-shabby-chic': slightly frayed but wonderfully authentic. Samode Haveli ranks as the perfect introduction to Jaipur. From the dining room, with its extraordinary blue-painted walls that have clearly inspired a textile designer or two, to the popular mirrored romantic fantasy of suite 114, this city palace gives the visitor the most precious experience of all: direct access to the legend of India.

---

address Samode Haveli, Gangapole, Jaipur, 302002 Rajasthan, India

telephone (91) 141 632 407 / 141 631 942 / 141 631 068 **fax** (91) 141 631 397

room rates from US$58 (including breakfast)

samode bagh

Sleeping in a tent in Rajasthan is nothing new: it's part of the folklore. The legendary Mughal ruler Shah Jahan, builder of the Taj Mahal, used to spend almost as much time in his tent as he did in his palaces. Hunting was a passion for this ruler, and he would go walkabout with his tent (and his entourage) for up to six months at a time. As you might imagine, we are not talking about a bolt of fabric and half a dozen poles. Shah Jahan's tent was more like a mobile palace than a hastily constructed temporary shelter. It was vast enough to accommodate his favourite wives, ministers, servants and warriors alongside, and it was opulent beyond imagination. The Shah's personal apartment featured walls of red velvet heavily embroidered with (real) gold and silver thread. The panels dividing the various spaces were cut to resemble Mughal arches. There were even chambers set aside for the conduct of government business.

Since Shah Jahan's tent was found virtually intact in the basement of Jodhpur's Meherangarh Fort, it has been a great asset to the study of India's Mughal heritage. Besides their passion for hunting and the compulsion to disappear at regular intervals, the other chief obsession of Mughal rulers was their gardens.

Paradise and garden in Arabic are the same word, and Mughal culture adopted the status of the Islamic garden wholeheartedly.

With such a legacy it is no surprise to see tents emerge in Rajasthan as an alternative to conventional hotel accommodation. They are particularly suited to the desert climate. Rajasthan is a semi-arid zone, and it only rains in the time of the monsoon, if at all. Nights are cool and days are dry and hot. Between September and April, when Samode Bagh is open, there is no chance of having to slop around in mud, or being woken by drips falling on your head, or any of the other familiar discomforts of tents in more temperate regions. But never mind history and climate, the chief reason for sleeping in a tent should be to experience the wild, just as it was for Shah Jahan. To wake up in a place without buildings or traffic – that for me is the most important ingredient of staying at Samode Bagh. Here is a chance to experience the natural beauty of Rajasthan in an environment that is Mughal with a capital M. Situated three miles from the village of Samode in a remote corner of Rajasthan set between craggy hills, sand dunes and savanna is the pleasure garden that belongs to the Samode Palace.

This is where descendants of the Samode royal family came for more than four centuries to enjoy the cool shade of magnificent trees, the soothing spectacle of intricate marble fountains and the carnival of elaborate family weddings and other gala events. Once upon a time many maharajas kept such pleasure gardens, but like all royal properties, they required strenuous and costly maintenance. This is one of the few that has survived – and it is beautifully intact.

As befits such a grand setting, Samode Bagh's tents are hardly ordinary. Inside, their fabric walls are decorated to mimic the famous murals in the Samode Palace. The furniture is Raj-era in inspiration, and beyond a flap at the back of the tent is a luxuriously appointed bathroom. But this is nothing compared to what awaits you when you step outside. The tents are arranged along the old boundary wall of a vast leafy space dominated by a centrally placed pavilion. At one end of this pleasant enclosure is a small, discreet staircase. Climb this and you will find yourself confronted by one of the most memorable visual experiences of Rajasthan: the exquisite Samode gardens, built more than four hundred years ago by Rawal Sheo Singhji. The vista includes marble arches, elaborate fountains, raised pavilions, sculpted trees, vines, shrubs, flowers and immaculate lawns. Interconnecting marble fountains fed by natural springs stretch away from you for two hundred feet with extraordinary geometric precision.

The gardens reveal themselves slowly. Behind a wall of *jali*, the traditional screen of carved stone fretwork, is a swimming pool as finely decorated as any porcelain plate. Each stretch of lawn set into its own sunken space is designated for a different activity: croquet, badminton, and so on. In the tradition of a Mughal campsite, activity is the order of the day. You can take a horse (or for that matter a camel) to explore the desert, then after a morning's ride you can retreat to the cool marble and foliage of the Samode garden, just as the maharajas used to do.

address Samode Bagh, Fatehpura Village (Bansa), Dist. Jaipur, Rajasthan, India
telephone (91) 141 630 943 / 141 631 942/ 141 632 407   **fax** (91) 141 631 397
room rates from US$58 (including breakfast)

atelier sul mare

Antonio Presti has a refreshing view on art. He's convinced that to be truly able to appreciate art you shouldn't just look at it, you need to *live* with it – it has to become part of your life. It's no wonder, Presti laments, that so many people dismiss modern art as emperor's new clothes, when the amount of time even an exhibition-goer spends with each painting, sculpture or installation can usually be measured in seconds. A self-confessed art fanatic, Presti long ago decided to do something about this. He used his family construction and cement fortune to build a sculpture park in the Sicilian hills half way between Palermo and Messina. The artworks he installed at Fiumara d'Arte are so convincingly monumental that the local authorities wanted to know why he had not paid his taxes on these houses…

Given his convictions, his next step was quite logical. He acquired a run-down hotel in a little village on Sicily's northern coast and set about transforming it into an art experience. The bar is the old garage, covered inside and out – at his invitation – in graffiti. Most of the lobby is taken up by a giant kiln for firing painted pottery, an activity in which guests are encouraged to participate. The reception is decorated with wall-to-wall press clippings (his own), and fourteen of the forty rooms were handed over to different artists to interpret individually. The result has deservedly generated enough worldwide press to cover several more walls in clippings. There is a comprehensiveness to the concept here that you will not find anywhere else in the world. The commitment to the art is total. Each room is an art installation that you can sleep in. One is covered – floor, walls, ceiling and even bed – in broken shards of coloured terracotta pots. Another, called 'The Sea Denied', is panelled throughout with old doors, some of which open to reveal closets and a bathroom, with a line of video screens showing continuous looped footage of waves rolling onto a shore.

For unrivalled originality and completeness of experience, the room Presti created himself as a homage to his favourite author is unsurpassed. The Pasolini Suite starts with a bang – literally. When you turn the key in the lock, the steel-plated door crashes to the floor. Talk about breaking the door down! A hidden steel cable pulls it back into position ready for its next victim. Kids love it – they will play with the front door all day long. It's a suitable prelude to the bathroom, called 'The Car Wash',

where a mess of copper pipes sprays water in every direction. This hilarious commemoration of Pasolini's tragic death in a car accident beats a morose headstone any day. In the bedroom itself, the walls and floors are covered in red mud, with Pasolini's words inscribed in Arabic below the ceiling. Why? Because the poet-director's favourite country was the Yemen. If the purpose of art – as legendary graphic artist Milton Glaser used to say – is to make you look at something differently, then Atelier sul Mare has certainly succeeded. There's a cerebral interactivity to everything here that can and probably will change your ideas on hotels as well as on art. Who would ever imagine, for example, that an all-white, egg-shaped concrete room with a mattress covered in fake stitched cotton feathers would be equally popular with art aficionados and art virgins? At Atelier sul Mare, Presti has well and truly proven his point. People who normally have little exposure to the world of contemporary art seem to enjoy staying here most of all. For once they can experience art and react to it any way they like – no pressure from a gallery owner prompting you to say something nice because you are drinking his champagne, no costly catalogues to make you revere the work, and no pretentious artspeak reviews telling you what to think of it. At Atelier sul Mare you live with the art – after that, how you feel about it is up to you. Nothing to buy, no-one to convert.

But with no disrespect to the artists, there is more to Atelier sul Mare than the art. It's located in the small fishing village of Castel di Tusa, immediately adjacent to the crystal clear warm waters of the Mediterranean. Here you can enjoy during the day the best that Sicily has to offer – a swim in the morning, fresh fish for lunch, an afternoon siesta and an evening of *passeggio* in the old square of the nearby town.

As for Signor Presti, he's busy as always dreaming up new schemes. Next on the agenda is a room installation by the Dalai Lama, set to be completed before summer 2001.

---

address Atelier sul Mare, via Cesare Battisti 4, Castel di Tusa, Messina, Sicily, Italy

telephone (39) 0921 334 295 **fax** (39) 0921 334 283

room rates from 105,000 Lira (including breakfast)

locanda dell'amorosa

The landscape between Mount Cetona and the valley below Sinalunga is an endless series of gently rolling hills dotted with cypress pines and small olive groves. This is an area that has been inhabited and cultivated since the time of the Etruscans. By local standards, therefore, the medieval hilltop village of Amorosa is a relative youngster. But the fact that it featured on a map printed in Antwerp in 1573 indicates that by that time it played a significant role in the area.

Amorosa is a typical fortified medieval estate or *fattoria* arranged around a small central piazza, with a watchtower, an owner's villa, a chapel, and a great assortment of residential and agricultural buildings. Wine and olives were produced here, and historically everyone who worked on the *fattoria* also lived here. Such was the tradition of the Tuscan village – a tradition that remained unchanged until remarkably recently. But in the nineteen-fifties and sixties the villages of Tuscany began to suffer for the first time the steady exodus to the cities and the United States that has long drained the population from rural areas further south. The land, not to mention an entire way of life, was in danger of being abandoned for good.

To a degree, rescue for Tuscany came in the form of tourism. This involved not only the arrival of wealthy English and German visitors, seduced by abandoned farmhouses in idyllic settings, but also agricultural tourism, whereby traditional farms offer accommodation in the summer months to help make ends meet. Contrary to rumour, Tuscany today is not overrun by tourism; if anything, it is preserved by it, and Locanda dell'Amorosa is a prime example of how that can happen.

When Carlo Citterio, a disillusioned advertising executive from Milan, first made the decision to up stakes and move to Amorosa twenty-five years ago, the tiny medieval village was no more than an assortment of empty buildings in varying stages of ruin. What had been a typically prosperous village in the Tuscan countryside, with a stable population of a couple of hundred, had degenerated into an uninhabited, dilapidated mess. This 'mess' was Citterio's by inheritance, and at the time it was far from clear that this was a fortuitous acquisition. Citterio began by establishing a restaurant in what were once the stables, and then slowly, over the years, undertook the reclamation of the village … one building at a time.

The view from the gatekeeper's cottage gives a glimpse of the grand manor house across the cobbled street

In July the fields surrounding Locanda dell'Amorosa are ablaze with the vivid yellow of sunflowers, grown for their oil

A handsome port with a wrought-iron gate was the entrance to the master's villa, the only noble house in the village

Everywhere, the patina of age makes this an unforgettably authentic experience

A cypress-lined drive leads up to the front gates of the hilltop town of Locanda dell'Amorosa

Owner Carlo Citterio's ancient family crest appears above the doors to the cellars

Certain parts of the old village haven't been touched at all yet, only adding to the charm and mystery of the place

The old stables house the restaurant, breakfast is served in the wine cellars and lunch in the garden – viva variety!

The bathrooms, like the guest rooms, are all different. This one belongs to the gatekeeper's cottage

Ambience and atmosphere are what you get at Amorosa. It was put together not by a decorator but by the hand of time

The cypress pine – enduring symbol of the rich heritage and Arcadian landscape of Tuscany

Whitewashed walls, terracotta floors, and the odd armchair upholstered in faded chintz create an aristocratic ambience

The window from the gatekeeper's tower looks straight back down the cypress-lined drive

These beautifully carved and gracefully aged stone steps belong to the manor house that is part of the village

Locanda dell'Amorosa is a medieval hilltop village converted in its entirety to accommodation for paying guests

The restoration was restrained: some peeling paint and splintered wood were allowed to stay that way

The estate includes its own vineyard, and the local vintage is taken very seriously

Colour, texture, patina – these are the visual qualities that Locanda dell'Amorosa has in abundance

The village of Amorosa is probably very close in appearance now to how it would have been four or five hundred years ago. But it is very, very different in how it functions. Today, the village is a hotel and the hotel is a village. At Locanda dell'Amorosa your room might equally be the watchtower, or the clock tower or the old laundry. And it goes on. The only building in the village where you wouldn't be offered a bed is the chapel. Throughout the two decades plus that he has devoted to the renovation, Citterio has focused intensely on preserving the spiritual as well as the structural integrity of the village. This is not one of those places where a whole collection of different buildings are united internally by a single design theme. Far from it. Just as there are no two spaces alike at Locanda dell'Amorosa, so there are no two matching design schemes.

One of the most charming aspects of Amorosa is the fact that it's not finished. Nor does Citterio think it ever will be – not, in any case, in his lifetime. There is a relaxed pace to the reclamation of the old buildings that feels in harmony with the agricultural rhythm of the land, and also seems to suit him particularly well. The promise of what the unrenovated buildings hold in store is every bit as rewarding as the reality of the ones that are finished. It would not be financially feasible to tackle them all at once, but in any case there is something indefinably romantic about being able to stroll through the surrounding vineyards and stumble across an abandoned farmhouse. Amazingly, the grandest building in the village, the old landowner's villa, has not been touched … yet. Last time I stayed, it was still being used to dry the laundry. Picture it: dripping white sheets hanging below elaborately painted Renaissance ceilings. How Italian!

Finally, this being Tuscany, it would be remiss of me not to mention the food. Suffice to say that Amorosa's restaurant, the one Citterio opened before he touched any other buildings, has made quite a name for itself. And in Tuscany that's really saying something.

address Locanda dell'Amorosa, Localita L'Amorosa, 53048 Sinalunga, Siena, Tuscany, Italy

telephone (39) 0577 679 497 **fax** (39) 0577 632 001

room rates from 369,000 Lira (including breakfast)

the caves

Negril, a former port frequented by pirates and slave traders, has in recent years emerged as one of Jamaica's most idyllic beachside resorts. It is blessed with an unbroken, seven-mile stretch of pure white sand as well as an environmental movement that is actively committed to keeping it that way. Less romantic sounding and certainly less well known than nearby Montego Bay, Negril is better qualified to fulfil the 'white beach, green water, blue sky' dreams of most visitors to a Caribbean island. Yet despite stricter controls on development and better planning, Negril itself is still no more than a succession of hotels parading alongside a postcard-perfect beach…pleasant, certainly, but not unique.

Not so The Caves, just a few miles along the coast. Perched on craggy cliffs thirty feet above a translucent emerald green sea, this hotel is unique in the Caribbean. It is a small jungle-clad retreat of thatched timber huts that literally sit on top of and in between some of the most spectacular sea caves in the world. These enormous caverns have been gouged out by the sea over aeons from the volcanic rock of the honeycomb cliffs below. The occasional cave even breaks through the surface above, like a massive skylight in the

middle of the property's ten virgin acres, and if you're game you can jump into the crater and splash into a subterranean pool thirty feet below. These half-submerged grottos are an extension of the coral reef system, and hence are filled with the inhabitants of the reef: eels, parrot fish, sponges, sea fans, rays and sea urchins. Some of the caves are large enough to take boats into, and of course it's a paradise for diving and snorkelling. Equipment is all included in the room rates; all you have to do is launch yourself into the twenty-foot waters below. Everywhere, platforms jut out over the water and steps are cut in the stone. You choose the height to jump from according to experience, courage or sheer recklessness. Acapulco-style cliff-diving is very much the order of the day. To the adventurous-spirited, all these panoramic little perches are like a siren constantly beckoning you to jump into the clear green waters below; to the rest of us they are perfect spots for soaking up the Caribbean sun.

The monumental subterranean caves of Negril, memorable enough in their own right, are just part of an experience that is totally Jamaican. From the custom-designed hand-made wooden furniture to the colourful fabrics

The sea caves of Negril are renowned as one of Jamaica's best spots for snorkelling and diving

In style the Caves hotel is a colourful blend of colonial, tribal and local craft influences

Brightly painted wooden fretwork creates privacy throughout the cliffside compound

The Caves restaurant is in a thatched pavilion perched on the edge of a cliff over a huge semi-submerged cave

Facing Mexico – thus due west – the Caves benefit from spectacular sunsets

Guests are housed in individual thatched huts, most with views over the Caribbean

and local works of art, this tropical cliffside retreat is stamped with the signature of the two artists who designed, built, and now operate it. When Bertram and Greer Ann Saulter, a committed Rastafarian couple, first moved to Negril it was to escape the city life of Kingston. At that time Negril was an uninhabited virgin piece of coastal jungle that counted a lighthouse as its only official building. There were no schools, no shops, and no tourists. It was so isolated, in fact, that most of their eight children were educated at home. The story of the Caves evolved out of their longstanding friendship with Chris Blackwell, founder of Island Records and a contemporary from their days in Kingston. Accepting the inevitability of Negril's emergence as a resort, and following Blackwell's example in turning to hotel development, they set out to create a low-key, environmentally friendly retreat.

Operating under the umbrella of Blackwell's growing stable of individual Island Outpost Hotels, the Caves is a three-dimensional expression of the Saulters' approach to life. Bertram designed and built the huts and the furniture, while Greer Ann created the interiors. The food is wholesome, tasty Jamaican fare, with an emphasis on fresh fish, Jamaican-style vegetables and tropical fruit. The rooms are cooled by shutters and ceiling fans (air conditioning, as far as the environment is concerned, is definitely *un*cool). The decor is dominated by bright colours and patterns. Reggae and blues are played in the thatched cliffside pavilion where meals are served. There are no televisions; evening entertainment consists of lively conversation enhanced by rum cocktails and the odd smoke.

For me there are two Jamaicas that capture the imagination, both irresistible. One is the colonial memory of steamer trunks, Noel Coward and 'white mischief'; the other is the colourful, laid-back, dreadlocked world of Bob Marley and reggae by the beach. The Caves perfectly captures this second, authentically Jamaican atmosphere.

---

address The Caves, Night House Road, PO Box 3113, West End, Negril, Jamaica

telephone (1 876) 957 0270   **fax** (1 876) 957 4930

room rates from US$213 per person (including all meals, drinks, sports and taxes)

portixol

'Here I am in Palma, amongst palm trees and cedars and olives and lemons and aloes and figs and pomegranates. The sky is turquoise blue, the sea is azure, the mountains are emerald green: the air is as pure as that of paradise. The sun shines all day long and it's warm and everybody wears summer clothes. At night one hears guitars and serenades.'

Those evocative lines were written by the composer Frédéric Chopin in a letter to Julien Fontana in 1838. So little has changed that it's no wonder Mikael and Johanna Landström couldn't bear to leave. Working for a Swedish hotel chain had introduced them to the island of Mallorca, and they had fallen heavily for the place. 'Living and working here became our goal. We loved the beauty, the culture and the international atmosphere. And of course as Swedes we couldn't help but be impressed by the weather.' Salvation came in the form of Portixol, a small hotel about a mile from the old town of Palma and only two hundred yards from the nearest beach. It had once had a reputation on the island as a great place to eat, but was now pretty run down. The new Swedish proprietors were undeterred. They took on a local architect, Rafael Vidal, and set out on the road to revitalization.

The look they ended up with was part accident, part design. They had a pale-wood, white-linen, pared-down Nordic feel in mind (no surprise), but what they got is 'new Spanish style' – an equally uncluttered ambience with contemporary furniture from Valencia and Barcelona, and teak bedheads and bookcases made to the couple's own designs. Original fifties furniture was renovated, the pool spruced up, and an unusual copper dome added to the restaurant (which is fast regaining its old reputation). Without question, however, the biggest drawcard of Portixol – aside from its affordability – is the location that inspired them to set it up in the first place.

Mallorca is very different from the other Balearic islands. Its extraordinary history goes right back to the Bronze Age, when the inhabitants erected great stone monuments bearing a remarkable resemblance to Stonehenge. Then came the Phoenicians, bringing with them their rich oriental culture. Mallorca was a convenient stop on the valuable purple-dye trade route, and they in turn introduced the islanders to fine silks and spices, and a high level of skill in weaving, ceramics, winemaking and gold- and silvercraft. In the process, Mallorca became one of the richest and most important islands in the Mediterranean. This was a fact not lost on the Romans, who, under the leadership of Quintus Caecilius Metellus, conquered Mallorca in 123 BC.

Metellus founded the city of Palma, and the island flourished under Roman rule. Not only did he build the signature Roman stone roads, but he also boosted the population by inviting 30,000-odd colonists to settle here. Even so, by the time the Moors arrived in AD 902, Mallorca had lapsed into a state of desolation. The ancient Roman cities were in ruins, reduced to mere fragments by raiders from north Africa, and the once rich agricultural economy was at a standstill.

The Moors successfully turned the situation around and went on to preside over four centuries of affluence. Theirs was the most enduring impact on the island's culture. Mallorcan Moors were known as the masters of the Mediterranean, and Palma under their rule was a well-organized, technologically advanced city dominated by a sophisticated Hispano-Arab upper class. So strongly was the Moorish influence embedded in the fibre of Mallorcan life that strenuous efforts by the subsequent Christian conquerors failed to eradicate it. With their Gothic cathedrals, all the new rulers did was add another layer to Mallorca's exotic collection of influences. By the 1600–1700s, Mallorca had once again established itself as a major centre for Mediterranean trade – so much so that Genoese merchants had set up a permanent exchange in Palma. The city now became one of the most important commercial centres for trade with India and Africa.

Several thousand years of intermittent wealth and war have given Mallorca, and Palma in particular, one of the most diverse cultures in the world, a unique blend of Arabesque, Italianate, Gothic, Oriental, Rococo, Renaissance and Baroque. It's an exotic place that can only be unveiled slowly. Palma, as George Sand noted, 'is not immediately revealed to the casual visitor.' At Portixol, you can afford to give it the time it deserves.

---

address Portixol, Calle Sirena 27, 07006 Palma de Mallorca, Spain

telephone (34) 971 27 18 00   **fax** (34) 971 27 50 25

room rates from 14,000 Pesetas (including breakfast)

Gone fishing!
Back in a minute.

PORTIXOL HOTEL Y RESTAURANTE

P·O·R·T·I·X·O·L

PISCINA

la tortuga

The Balearic islands of Formentera, Ibiza, Mallorca and Menorca share a common history of invaders and conquerors – including the Phoenicians, the Greeks, the Carthaginians, Romans, the Moors, and the Catalan Christians from Spain. Yet the islands themselves have always stayed diverse and individual. They are not a marked set, despite the fact that these days they all depend on tourism as their most important industry. Even the seven-odd million tourists a year have not affected the islands' distinct personalities. They may belong to the same archipelago, but as siblings they're virtually unrecognizable.

Formentera is small, dry and unremarkable in its history and in ambitions. Mallorca on the other hand is a mini-nation with a richly layered culture and a capital city among the Mediterranean's most impressive. Ibiza is the family comedian: a physically handsome island of *calas*, pine forests and white beaches that is, first and foremost, dedicated to hedonism. Then there's Menorca. This kidney-shaped island doesn't have the physical beauty of Mallorca or Ibiza, and its soil is nowhere near as fertile as that of its neighbours. The Menorcans, however, are quite candid and philosophical about their shortcomings. After

God was finished with Mallorca, they will tell you, St Peter was so inspired that he begged for a chance to create an island of his own. God consented and the result was Menorca. God could see, however, that St Peter hadn't exactly excelled himself and so in an effort to make good, He proposed to Peter that 'from now on you look after the Mallorcans and I'll take care of the Menorcans.' The moral of the story? Mallorca may be prettier but Menorcans have a better life.

If that sounds like a rather English piece of pragmatism, that would be because it probably is. Alone among the Balearic islands, Menorca was under British rule for almost a century, a period which has coloured the island quite distinctly. This is the only part of Spain where you're likely to find large houses of Palladian inspiration that resemble the country houses of Sussex, Kent and Dorset, and are filled with Queen Anne and Chippendale furniture. The only real difference is their colour. These stately piles were painted a deep shade of rust, apparently because that was the colour the British navy painted their ships below the waterline; in other words, it was the only paint around. The Menorcans' fanatical devotion to their horses also betrays British influence.

They race them enthusiastically and show them off in the island's grand fiestas. The British also introduced dairy farming and today, Menorca's Mahon cheese is made on both an industrialized scale and a farmhouse scale and eaten all over Spain. Even the language didn't escape English influence. On Menorca the colloquial phrase for 'a few people' is *una jane y un boy*.

It isn't hard to understand how someone can come to this island and never want to leave. It may not be as spectacular as Mallorca or as sexy as Ibiza, but it more than makes up for it in charm. The ambience is like that of a village on the west coast of Ireland – only with *much* better weather. Accordingly, most people are now far more attracted to the seaside villages of whitewashed stone houses with their terracotta roofs and bougainvillaea creepers than to the fading, crumbling, red-brown Palladian mansions left behind by the colonials. One such village is San Luis, the famous 'white village' south of the town of Mahon that was once the seat of the island's French government (everyone had a turn in the Balearics, including the French in the mid-eighteenth century, when the British were ever-so-briefly kicked out).

Belgian fashion photographer Karel Fonteyne came to the island to do a shoot and couldn't bear to leave. Instead, he acquired a series of small stone houses and slowly, doing most of the work himself, converted them into a collection of jewel-like coloured spaces that function as a small, exquisite hotel. The interiors are just what you might expect from a person who used to look through a lens all day: artfully arranged, incredibly colourful and wholly unpredictable in their mix of the unexpected and the everyday. They are like giant, three-dimensional still lifes, and one senses that Fonteyne is happiest experimenting with and rearranging his creations. This is the kind of place you dream of finding: creative, charming, colourful, comfortable – in other words completely in step with the island itself.

---

address La Tortuga, Apartado Correyos 87, Alaior, Menorca, Spain

telephone (34) 9713 724 81   **fax** (34) 9713 724 81

room rates from 16,000 Pesetas (including breakfast)

caravanserai

A caravanserai was where camel trains would stop to rest and stock up on supplies as they worked their slow way up the oasis route through the Sahara to Marrakesh; it makes a good name for a hotel. Marrakesh was a town mixing cultures centuries before it became a style trend. Traders there exchanged African slaves, gold, jewelry and nuts for cloth, oil, and manufactured goods from Europe.

Mixing cultures, or more accurately the design signatures of different cultures, was exactly what Max Lawrence and Stephane Boccara had in mind when they first came up with the idea of this hotel. As the son of parents who travelled for a living, Max had seen quite a bit of the world and, as could perhaps be expected, a place in England was not for him. He came to Morocco after completing school, and never left. One of the first friends he made there was Stephane Boccara, son of one of Morocco's best-known architects, Charles Boccara. Stephane went off to Paris to study architecture and returned determined *not* to follow in his father's footsteps. Instead he decided to become a client, choosing to get involved in property development, and in particular in the development of hotels. Max Lawrence by then had considerable

experience in renovating riads in the old medina of Marrakesh. With complementary skills – one creative, one practical – they decided to join forces.

What they wanted to create was a place grounded in ethnic character but not necessarily purely Moroccan. It was to mix the whitewashed aesthetic of Greece, the colours of India and the courtyard architecture of the Mediterranean; the furnishings were to have the seductive appeal of handcraft, whether Rajasthani, Nepalese or Moroccan.

As it happened, Boccara senior had just the venue for this ethno-chic project. Long before Marrakesh began its recent expansion (the city now counts more than a million inhabitants) he had purchased practically an entire village on the fringe of the city's palm-studded hinterland. Architecturally, it was nothing much: just a cluster of small huts built in the traditional way out of compacted mud. But this Berber village had a great location and real ethnic credentials. It was perfect as the starting point for Caravanserai. Max and Stephane negotiated to acquire the site and their multicultural dream started to take shape.

Architecturally, their vision was clear. People staying here would not just get a room.

Antique Moroccan painted bridal chests are part of the multicultural assemblage that defines Caravanserai

Countless carved Moroccan doors continually lead from one hidden space to another

The roof terrace, which borrows from a Greek tradition, overlooks the Palmerai and the Atlas mountains

n converting this old Berber village into a hotel, tremendous care was taken to preserve texture and character

One of the guest suites has a mini-Majorelle garden painted in the distinctive Majorelle shade of blue

Another suite with a private pool (below) also comes with a spacious hammam or steam room

caravanserai

Guests at Caravanserai would each get their own small house equipped with a collection of spaces every bit as eclectic and unexpected as the ethno-artifacts decorating them. Thus you might find yourself in a suite (for want of a more suitable word) featuring a private garden painted Majorelle blue, an expansive bathroom opening onto the garden, and a series of other discrete spaces including a small bedroom and a study. Another suite has a small private pool in a small private courtyard, off which lie a bedroom and separate study, an entrance hall, and a bathroom that happens to be equipped with an enormous private hammam (the traditional Moroccan steam room). The bedroom has beautiful vaulted ceilings and a traditional fireplace.

While the design approach is authentically multicultural, the ingredients of Caravanserai are in fact largely Moroccan. Its architectural concept owes a lot to the Berber village, which is traditionally full of unexpected courtyards, terraces and hidden spaces. And its building

techniques and materials have been used in southern Morocco for centuries. Wooden frames are constructed on either side of an existing wall, and then damp earth stamped on top of it, compacted and allowed to dry. This is a system that offers great insulation as well as aesthetic character. It doesn't fare well in heavy rain, but that's not too much of a problem in Morocco.

Extraordinarily, each collection of rooms and spaces still costs less than an average hotel room. From the very beginning, the intention was to make this particular Moroccan experience affordable. Now that it's finished, it's a pleasure to be able to announce that they have achieved all their aims. Caravanserai really lives up to its name. The look is a seductive tribal blend, the spaces are at once generous yet mysterious and contained, the variety of accommodation is amazing, and the location is romantic and unspoiled. All in all, it creates the powerful impression that time here has stood still – even if you know it's not true.

address Caravanserai, Ouled Ben Rahmoun, Marrakesh, Morocco
telephone (212) 61 24 98 98 **fax** (212) 44 43 71 60
room rates from 1,260 Dhs

174

kasbah ben moro

It's known as the road of a thousand kasbahs: a long thin sliver that starts in the frontier town of Ouarzazate and extends into the seemingly infinite desert of Morocco's southern Sahara. Just twenty miles along the way you reach the ancient oasis town of Skoura. Here the famous caravanserai, the trading camel trains, would stop for supplies and one final rest before embarking on the arduous crossing of the mighty Atlas mountains en route to their destination of Marrakesh.

This is the land of Paul Bowles's novel *The Sheltering Sky*. It's remote, hot and exotic. By day it's blanketed in a crystal clear purple-blue sky; by night in a deep black star-studded sky. The lush palm grove of Skoura contains many fine examples of the mud castles of southern Morocco that have inspired countless artists, writers and travellers. Most of these fascinating structures, with their distinctively shaped towers and graphic chiselled detailing, are in a state of ruin: impressive, enthralling, like nothing else you have ever seen, but sadly uninhabitable. All, that is, except one. The Kasbah Ben Moro, in the middle of the Skoura Palmerai, has been restored to the condition it was in when first built by a Spaniard in the late eighteenth century.

By a twist of fate, the resurrection of this splendid Moroccan fantasy has come about by the energy and enthusiasm of another Spaniard, Don Juan de Dios Romero Muños. Juan used to visit Morocco regularly. A passionate off-road motorcyclist, he was well acquainted with the striking landscape that begins on the far side of the Atlas Mountains from Marrakesh. But I doubt he believed that he would one day live here, much less that he would rescue a piece of the region's extraordinary architectural history. He worked as a bank manager in Cadiz, and although he has Andalusian blood in his veins, he was an unlikely candidate to say goodbye to his day job and embark on a Sahara adventure. Yet that's exactly what he did. Fed up with modern Spain, in the late 1990s he upped stakes and moved to Ouarzazate.

He had found and fallen hopelessly in love with the dilapidated ruin of a once proud kasbah, and he was determined to restore it. All that stood in his way were the fifty-four relatives who owned the property. Undeterred, he decided to stay in Ouarzazate for as long as necessary to get all of them to agree to sell. It took six months for the eleven representatives of all the clans to sign an official document.

Simple details like this wall lamp set the atmosphere – dark, exotic and very Moroccan

This is the traditional territory of Berbers, the fiercely proud and independent nomads of north Africa

Every detail, right down to the carved wooden door hinges, was remade to authentic patterns

The restored Kasbah Ben Moro is one of the finest examples of Morocco's famous fortress architecture

In the pitch black of night, the labyrinthine mud architecture has a spooky atmosphere

Such massive and imposing kasbahs were meant to impress friends and enemies – but especially enemies

At the very core of the courtyards is a multi-storey lightwell with numerous arched openings

The landscape is the same colour as the kasbah itself – not surprising, given that they are both of the same material

Dark, mysterious, even a bit scary, this is the Morocco of Paul Bowles's *The Sheltering Sky*

Inside, Kasbah Ben Moro is an Escher-like structure of courtyards within courtyards within courtyards

The symbols, shapes and building materials define a centuries-old architectural tradition

The bleak and unforgiving landscape en route to the kasbah makes the lush Skoura Palmerai even more inviting

The bedrooms are simple but handsome. Furniture, accessories and detailing are all authentically Berber

The oasis of Skoura is a vast expanse of palm trees framed by the snow-capped Atlas mountains and the Sahara desert

Even the twisting staircase is an exotic experience, complete with handcrafted bronze balustrade and hidden spaces

Despite its remoteness, the restaurant, in the yellow and maroon colours of southern Morocco, is surprisingly good

The four-hundred-year-old kasbah was restored with minute attention to original detail

Once upon a time, a constant lookout was kept from the watchtowers for the new arrival of travelling camel trains

Then finally Kasbah Ben Moro was his – or at least what was left of it was. Its elegant, noble outline was still discernible, but that was about all. None of the internal structure, which once housed the first Spaniard, plus wives, children and livestock, survived. It was clear that Juan had not just purchased a monumental building but a monumental project.

For two years he slept on site in a mud hut while he and his workmen set about rebuilding the kasbah exactly as it once was. Although the techniques of building in mud are slowly dying out, he managed to find enough tradesmen in the south of Morocco who were skilled in the traditional ways. His architectural blueprint and manifesto was the work of a photographer friend who had documented the most important kasbahs still standing in Morocco in a book filled with invaluable detail of everything from the construction of wooden hinges to the layout of spaces. This enabled Juan to achieve his goal of authenticity. As he enthusiastically points out, what he has created

– or rather recreated – is a vivid insight into ancient Morocco. Instead of exploring scattered ruins, here you eat and sleep in the real thing.

So what's it like to stay in a four-hundred-year-old mud castle? The word that comes to mind is quiet – dead quiet. Set in the middle of the Skoura oasis, framed by the snow-capped Atlas in the distance, the absolute absence of noise is a continual reminder of the proximity of the Sahara and the remoteness of everything else. At night it can feel a little spooky to be so gloriously situated in the middle of nowhere. The nearest town is Ouarzazate (an hour's drive) and Marrakesh is six hours away through the mountains. In designing the interiors, Juan focused on what was important and left out what was not. Rooms are simple but impressive and bathrooms are spacious and efficient. The food too is rather good – a surprise in such a remote setting. But above all, he didn't turn the place into something it never was. It really is again as it was when the camel trains pulled in four centuries ago. It's not plush, it's real.

address Kasbah Ben Moro, 45500 Skoura, Ouarzazate, Morocco

telephone (212) 44 85 21 16   **fax** (212) 44 85 20 26

room rates from 350 Dhs

riad kaiss

Not so long ago staying in the medina of Marrakesh – the medieval heart of Morocco's most exotic city – was not something a visitor could or probably would do. There were a few exceptions: riads, or inner city palaces, were acquired by the odd wealthy Western eccentric, such as Bill Willis, designer friend of the Gettys, or Mireille d'Arc, superstar French actress; but to most visitors, the medina remained out of bounds.

When Morocco became a French protectorate in 1912, its first governor Marshal Lyautey laid down the policy of the future colonial regime. The French, he specified, were 'not to touch a Moroccan hair or disturb a single Moroccan custom'. French settlers and the colonial bureaucracy were thus established in new neighbourhoods built outside the old city walls, and the medinas of Fez, Rabat, Meknès and Marrakesh were left undisturbed. Their inner networks of lanes, bazaars, workshops, and hidden courtyards remained as some of the most authentic medieval survivals in the world. Morocco had, after all, turned its back on the rest of the world for more than four hundred years after the collapse of Islamic rule in Andalusia. When the French took over, the country had no railways, no electricity, no sewerage, and no running water. Self-imposed isolation had preserved a way of life unchanged since the Middle Ages.

By the second half of the twentieth century this timewarp, complete with all the sounds, smells, and bustling activity of the medina experience, had become an irresistible lure to the adventurous, West-weary traveller. It was (and still is) a journey back to a pre-sanitized way of life. And in the case of Marrakesh, it is a journey into a city that since the thirteenth century has had a reputation as one of the most exotic on earth. This was where Europe and Africa met to trade in gold, spices and slaves. Even now that Morocco has cars, televisions, supermarkets, mobile phones, Pizza Huts and the internet, the Marrakesh medina still tempts and often overwhelms the unsuspecting Western visitor. It's a daily piece of fascinating urban theatre, a maze of shady alleys lined with tiny butchers' shops, carpenters' workshops, reeking dye works, shoemakers set up in impossibly small closet-like spaces, donkeys pulling carts that are only a few inches narrower than the streets, old men in hooded jellabas, modestly veiled women, and carpet merchants awaiting their next customer with fresh mint tea.

Guest rooms at Riad Kaiss are typically Moroccan with a distinctively modern, restrained edge

Situated between two rooms adjoining the courtyard is a small corridor with a magnificent fireplace

The main courtyard is an oasis of cool green calm – totally unexpected in the heart of Marrakesh's dense medina

Upstairs, overlooking the courtyard garden, are the grandest rooms of the palace, today used as a salon for guests

The bathrooms, like the rooms, are all different and yet all unmistakably Moroccan in materials, detail and design

Riad Kaiss has plenty of tucked-away spaces and hidden retreats, like this rooftop tea pagoda

riad kaiss

As the contrast between the old Morocco and the modern world becomes ever more pronounced, the attraction has only magnified. And these days visitors can't get enough of the intoxicating atmosphere of the medina. Whereas once a tourist would venture in only during the day with a guide (essential, by the way, because even the average local doesn't know his way around this huge labyrinth, which contains some 26,000 houses), now they also come for dinner to places like Yacout, a palace converted into an extraordinary restaurant. Many go one step further, turning traditional Moroccan tourism on its head by staying in the medina and taking the odd daytrip beyond the confines of the old walled city. Just a decade ago this was not possible – the option of staying in the medina, other than with friends, was simply unavailable. But in the past few years many Europeans have quite logically concluded that if an old riad can make a spectacular restaurant then it would probably work just as well or better as a hotel.

Moroccans themselves can't work it out. Why would anybody, let alone wealthy foreigners, choose to stay in the medina? It's cramped, there are no street signs, everybody gets lost, one dark laneway looks like the next, and it's aromatic (to put it most politely). Many medina residents dream of the suburban life they see on TV – but most of the incomers have had enough of exactly that.

There are riads and there are spectacular riads, but few are as palatial as Riad Kaiss. Situated at the end of a typically dark, typically narrow laneway, Kaiss is owned by French architect Christian Ferre, who used to design hotels in Asia. After early retirement, he too could not resist the pull of the medina's medieval mystique. Riad Kaiss has a grand tiled courtyard with fountains and mature trees, and beautifully ornate rooms with fireplaces and authentic decorative detail, all restored with the sure hand of a professional. You may even find yourself wishing they didn't have guides – then you'd have an excuse never to leave.

address Riad Kaiss, 65 Derb Jdid, Riad Zitoun Kedim, Marrakesh 40000, Morocco
telephone (212) 44 44 01 41 **fax** (212) 44 44 01 41
room rates from 1,100 Dhs (including breakfast)

villa maroc

Essaouira is the kind of place that's continually being discovered. Everyone who ends up here walks around with the expression of a cat that has caught a mouse. There's an unspoilt, authentic quality to this Moroccan Atlantic port that gives visitors the impression that it is an unexplored gem.

In fact, people have been discovering Essaouira since ancient times. It all started with the colour purple. The Romans tried to keep Mogador (as Essaouira was then known) a secret because they used an island off the coast to manufacture purple dye. More valuable than gold, this was the colour of rank and authority. It was understandably important to restrict access to its precious dye source.

The next empire to discover Mogador was Portuguese. The rich, seafaring Portuguese needed Atlantic ports of call for their merchant navy on the arduous but extraordinarily profitable passage to the Far East. They built Essaouira's formidable sea wall and defences, complete with strategically placed canons, all of which are perfectly intact today. Orson Welles, in search of an authentic Mediterranean trading town as a location for his famous film version of Othello, eventually settled upon Essaouira. It may not have been on the Med,

but it was better preserved than any of its Mediterranean counterparts. The town commemorates this most famous episode in its modern history with a statue dedicated to the great filmmaker in the main square.

But it's not just the legacy of this little seaside town that makes it so attractive; ambience also sets Essaouira apart. Many first-timers who come here on day excursions from Marrakesh are overwhelmed by the difference between the two. While Marrakesh is alive with hustling activity and furious intrigue, Essaouira is easy-going. Visitors are even left to their own devices in the market, sometimes to the point that you have to ask to buy something – an unheard of scenario in Marrakesh. This old trading post is a firm favourite with the surfing community, particularly windsurfers – one, because it always blows, and two, because it is eminently affordable. If Essaouira was laid-back before, the surfers have made it more so.

Still, beaches and surf are just one of the town's attractions. Essaouira maintains its centuries-old position as the woodworking capital of Morocco. This is an area plentifully supplied with argan trees, a source of excellent timber as well as the much-prized argan oil, a delicacy in Moroccan cuisine. All the signature varieties of Moroccan woodwork are produced here, particularly marquetry – decorative inlays of contrasting timber – and the deeply ingrained tradition of *moushrabiya*, the intricately patterned screens once used (not so long ago) to hide women from the eyes of men.

These days Essaouira is also well-known for the extraordinary range of alternative medicines and cosmetics available here. A plethora of rainbow-coloured lotions, potions and powders that solve everything (you hope) from pale lips to your libido (both ways) are available in a section of the market that looks like a Kodacolor version of a witch-doctor's convention. For those who are not enthusiasts of medicine-man medicine, the golden rule is: 'if you don't know what it is, don't ask'.

There are lots of accommodation options in this colourful town, from converted townhouses to a pitch for your tent. But the best two are Auberge Tangaro and Villa Maroc. Tangaro, just outside town and not far from the best windsurfing beach, is popular with the surfing

crowd. Villa Maroc, a converted Moorish mansion just inside the old city walls, draws the culture crowd. Everything Essaouira is famous for – cafés, shops, woodworkers, and those black-magic markets – is on your doorstep. Having said that, the closest beach is also only a stone's throw away – five minutes on foot at most. Inside, the beauty of Villa Maroc comes as a pleasant surprise. As an old nobleman's townhouse, it is predictably large, but you might not expect it to be so pretty or cosy. Like much Moroccan architecture, it has plenty of secluded spaces. So while everyone else has breakfast in the salon, you could choose to have your croissants, Moroccan pancakes and coffee in the sun on the roof terrace. Or in winter, when temperatures drop significantly at night, you might forgo the dining room for a romantic fireside dinner in the salon by the bar. How captivating is the charm of Essaouira? Enough to convince a couple who had never been to Morocco before to buy the house next door after just five days at Villa Maroc.

address Villa Maroc, 10 rue Abdellah Ben Yassin, Essaouira, Morocco

telephone (212) 44 47 31 47 **fax** (212) 44 47 28 06

room rates from 676 Dhs (including breakfast)

canal house hotel

Given what a popular destination Amsterdam is, it's surprising that the city has never produced any equally popular places to stay. Until recently, the choice was woeful. There was the really cheap, the really expensive and the really bland. There are plenty of youth hostels catering to the armies of backpackers, such as the famous Fat City in the red light district. At the opposite end of the scale there are Amsterdam's grand alternatives – big places with plenty of gold buttons and staff who say sir all the time. But they are not so grand by London or Paris standards, and they're certainly a bit anachronistic in such a hip and youthful city. As for bland: most of the large international chains like Radison, Meridien and Hilton are here if that's what you like.

It's all so frustrating when what people want from Amsterdam is so simple: like the Amsterdammers themselves, they want to stay on one of the canals. This is where all the city's charm, beauty and history are concentrated. Canal houses are the most sought-after and prestigious properties in this city. Unlike many other centres of old cities, this one has not been ruined by mass conversion to offices and the stifling atmosphere of a nine-to-five work environment. The centre of old Amsterdam is

as residential as it was seven centuries ago. And apart from cars parked along the waterfront, it doesn't look much different either. But this preservation was not by the grace of fortuitous fate. As you would expect of the Dutch, the survival of the city's dollhouse-like canalside architecture owes largely to a masterplan.

In the early 1960s, Amsterdam was steadily moving in the same direction as most old European cities – people were opting for the space and green of the suburbs, and companies were taking advantage of inexpensive inner-city real estate to convert once beautifully decorated residences into sterile offices. It was a trend that was threatening to destroy Amsterdam's picturesque charm. Luckily, city hall made a commitment to reverse the process before it was too late. They wanted people to live in the city and commute to office blocks on its outskirts. Most unusually for an inner-city council, they put their money where their mouth was. In the early seventies, to coincide with the city of Amsterdam's seven-hundredth anniversary, they launched a policy of refusing not only all new commercial lease applications for canal houses, but the renewal of existing ones. The message was clear – companies had to get out. To encourage the residents back,

town hall offered a guilder-for-guilder subsidy for renovation work, provided only that it had official approval. It worked a dream. Amsterdam centre reverted to residential use. People live in historic splendour along the canals in walking distance of all the bakeries, cafés, restaurants and shops that cater to an urban population. In the morning, many drive to ultramodern office complexes scattered on the outer perimeter of the city's ring road.

The authorities did a good job – maybe too good a job. Canal houses became so in demand that the chances of any ever operating as a hotel were slim. That's what makes the opportunity to stay in one so special, particularly one that hasn't been too tarted up. This is the beauty of the appropriately titled Canal House. Admittedly some of its decoration is on the tired side, but more important is that the spaces are intact. The breakfast room, for example, is an enormous ballroom with elaborately tall ceilings and a bank of elegant windows that overlook a walled garden

complete with gazebo. The survival of this kind of space in the centre of Amsterdam is almost unheard of; the fact that it is the hotel breakfast room flies in the face of any return-per-square-foot calculation. It's clear that there are purists at work here. You will find no minibar, no television, no plastic laundry bags, no chocolate on the pillow. What you do get is the real Amsterdam. Canal House is located on the Keizersgracht, the Emperor's Canal – the grandest of them all. Here you are within easy walking distance of all the most unusual boutiques and cosmopolitan restaurants. My favourite guest rooms are on the front of the building, not just because they overlook the canal but also because of their exposed beams and their quirky Art Nouveau and Deco furniture. There will doubtless be parts of Canal House you don't like (the modern lift, for example, or the slightly seventies bathrooms), but the fact that Canal House is a real canal house more than makes up for the odd decorative shortcoming.

address Canal House Hotel, Keizersgracht 148 1015 CX, Amsterdam, Netherlands
telephone (31) 20 622 5182 **fax** (31) 20 624 1317
room rates from 295 Guilders (including breakfast)

eivindsplass fjellgard

Who could fail to have been inspired by the 1994 Lillehammer winter Olympics? It was not just that the Norwegians were so hospitable and well-organized; what impressed me most was the beauty, the style and the appropriateness with which they put their buildings together. What a fantastic feat of imagination, for instance, to model the skating hall on an upside-down Viking ship. That's what I find so engaging about the Norwegians: as a result of their relative isolation and their harsh climate they have managed to maintain their cultural integrity. They may be a modern nation but they are not in conflict with any aspect of their heritage. The typical black and white snow-patterned woollen sweaters are not just still being made, they are still being worn, which says a lot more. Cross-country skiing is not just a sport but a part of the folklore (on a par with cricket in India and jogging in Los Angeles); the diet continues to be based on traditional staples like *flatbrød* and smoked fish; and, most visibly, the entire country retains its strong affinity with wood. Wooden boats, wooden barns, wooden floors, wooden churches, painted wooden furniture, carved wooden decoration: wood is an unmistakable design signature of Norway.

The Norwegian tradition of woodworking dates back to the Vikings. The longship was the engineering marvel of its day, and the Vikings were consummate woodworkers, not just in terms of construction, but in ornamental work as well. With forest covering most of the land, and long dark winters in which to spend many hours indoors, woodworking skills were passed from father to son. Cooking vessels, tools, beds, cupboards, sleds – in fact the whole home and everything in it were made by the man of the house. Self-reliance in woodworking skills was taken for granted. Even today, the Norwegian woodmen of the north have a saying that goes 'any man who can't do everything is an idiot'.

Much has been written about the persuasive peasant style indigenous to Norway, and if anything interest in Norwegian style is on the increase. Eivindsplass Fjellgard is its perfect embodiment. Situated six miles from the village of Geilo, one of the oldest and best-known winter resorts in Norway, the hotel consists of a collection of authentic wooden huts that were salvaged from all over the region and reassembled in their new location. Eivindsplass Fjellgard not only preserves architecture that might otherwise have perished, it creates an opportunity to stay in it.

eivindsplass fjellgard

There is just one vital difference: in addition to being authentic these huts are also insulated, which they were certainly not in their original state. It's a discreet and permissible modern intrusion. Aside from this slight adjustment, the huts are all decorated in the traditional Norwegian style. The most captivating element is their resplendent *rosemaling*. When, in the mid-eighteenth century, hand-hewn logs on interior walls began to be replaced by sideboarding and plastering, handpainted decoration by rural artists started to flourish. This vivid art form very quickly became established as a popular and enduring Norwegian folk tradition. The name *rosemaling* literally means 'rose painting', and it describes the flowering vines and other motifs that trail over walls, ceilings, doors and window frames, cupboards, chests, benches and beds. Not only was Norwegian wooden furniture richly carved, it was now also ablaze with colour. Added to the ubiquitous hearth, a generous fireplace of riverstone covered in

decorative stucco, the colour, the detail, the character and the patina of these huts make for a captivating experience.

As can be expected from our efficient northern neighbours, the arrangement of the huts is well organized. A larger central building houses the reception, the restaurant and the kitchen, while the smaller huts are positioned around it. Every hut, naturally enough, is different in size and configuration, but what they all have in common is the authenticity of the Norwegian rural tradition.

On the north rim of the Hardangervidda, one of the largest mountain plateaus in Europe, this hotel affords a chance to step into the picturesque Norway of coffee-table books. Norma Skurka, an American author with roots in Norway, summed it up best: 'With their gay abandon and flamboyant colours, Norway's folk arts and log buildings carry a message to the modern world not to abandon the quiet basics, the courageous boldness and spirit of joy inherent in simple rural existence.'

address Eivindsplass Fjellgard, 3580 Geilo, Norway
telephone (47) 32 094845 **fax** (47) 32 09 48 24
room rates from 670 NOK

club med bora bora

I've never been a big fan of the Club. Sure they have some spectacular sites, but all that emphasis on group activity makes them a bit too much like a cruise ship that doesn't move. Moreover, I've never been a big fan of audience participation. OK, I might get up and jiggle with a belly dancer in a Moroccan restaurant, but that's where I draw the line. A two-week Club Med holiday pushes me right over it. Fourteen days of working out how many pink beads equals one imported beer. A fortnight of declining to participate in twenty-three different varieties of silly adult games. Half a month of having to eat with people who never stop eating simply because the food, like Mount Everest, is there…

But when I heard that Christian Liaigre was designing a Club Med on the island of Bora Bora, things started to look up. Even Club Med, I thought, couldn't mess up a magical combination like Liaigre and Polynesia – and I was right. Hiring M. Liaigre, the master of luxurious minimalism, to dream up an aesthetic scheme for an idyllic location was pure inspiration. What is needed in paradise, after all, is very little. But it is no easy task to determine what that little should be. As a designer Liaigre is a thinker. His work is above

all concerned with identifying and reinventing the ingredients, materials, and symbols that make a particular place distinctive. That's how, for instance, his famous Twig stool came about. It has a Robinson Crusoe, 'I made this while I was roasting my fish' look about it, but the form, workmanship and proportion still spell French precision and craftsmanship. It's the perfect combination of rustic and refined. The same applies to the Club Med door handles. A fish may be a predictable motif for an island resort, but an abstract fish fashioned in cast bronze transports it from the realms of kitsch to those of barefoot artist. Ditto for the nautilus shells with which Liaigre decorated the lobby: again, a bit of a cliché, but not when they are positioned on brackets inspired by those that held up the finest clocks in eighteenth-century Parisian salons. Even something as mundane as the room numbers has Liaigre's subtle and culturally appropriate signature. They were carved into traditional Polynesian hardwood canoe paddles, which were then speared handle end into the ground.

What Club Med got at Bora Bora, even if it's not quite what they are known for, was a very sophisticated and subtle style. Ironically, this Liaigre venture is in some senses a return

to roots for this huge travel company. Club Med started up just after World War II with army surplus tents. They were cheap, they were simple, and they were pitched in amazing locations. The concept too was simple – the point was to get away from all the nonsense of travel, from the luggage which used to weigh a ton, from the letters of credit (don't forget this was fifty years ago), and from all the people in gold buttons and pill-box hats. At Club Med, you didn't need any of that. What you did need didn't add up to more than a swimsuit, a snorkel and a sweater. For its day, it was very minimal, very daring and very popular. Sadly, along the way the group lost its simplicity and its purity.

So considering where Club Med came from, Christian Liaigre wasn't such an unlikely choice after all. Some cynics have suggested that everything looks good in paradise, but one peek inside the average hotel in Tahiti will convince you otherwise. Bora Bora got a complete makeover. No detail was overlooked,

no surface spared. The plates have ocean blue spiral patterns ubiquitous in Polynesian culture, the espresso cups a tribal stick man in brown. The dining area has colonial-inspired teak chairs, columns were clad in totem shapes, pebbles arranged in traditional patterns were set into the polished concrete floors, sidetables and even beach showers echo the lashing of traditional tools. It's an impressive body of work. But does it make a difference? Is this Club Med less of a circus – or is it same circus, different tent? The answer is better circus, better tent. Group activity and audience participation do take place, but in a more restrained fashion. If you opt not to participate, you won't be the bad apple. More importantly, this Club Med has made a name on the island of Bora Bora as *the* place to hang out, even though some of the other resorts are far more exclusive and far more expensive. Oh, and they got rid of those silly beads … and replaced them with coloured shells. How many pink ones was that for a Heineken?

---

address Club Med Bora Bora, BP 34 Anau, Vaitape, Bora Bora, French Polynesia

telephone (689) 604 604 **fax** (689) 604 611

room rates from FF 5,800 (per week including all meals and sports)

convento de santo antónio

Like the Spanish government with their Paradores, the Portuguese have done a fabulous job of converting the country's many fine but now largely anachronistic historic properties into very stylish hotels. The Pousadas, as they are called, offer the best of all worlds: impressive history, modern comforts, and affordable rates. The problem however is that Pousadas are very thin on the ground in the Algarve, and yet that's where everyone wants to go – at least everyone who's not Portuguese. This southern stretch of Portuguese coastline is blessed with what may be the best climate in Europe. It's warm in the winter, not too hot in the summer and it seldom rains. For northern Europeans accustomed to six or seven months of grey a year it's paradise. But a lot of it can be paradise without a soul: miles and miles of characterless buildings that can be visual hell for the unsuspecting tourist.

One big exception is Tavira. Situated on either side of the River Gião, its two halves linked by two low, old bridges, this town of church spires (twenty-seven of them, to be exact) has been able to maintain its identity as an old fishing port. As the first port of call after Morocco, Tavira was a vital player during Portugal's expansion period, and was at one time the sixth-largest city in Portugal. Positioned between the the hills and the coastal marshes, Tavira is one of the very few towns in the Algarve that retain the appearance they acquired in ancient times, with the odd Roman bridge, a cobbled medieval centre, and a healthy sprinkling of Muslim influence. Indeed the name Algarve stems from the Moorish period: it derives from the Arabic 'El Garb Andalus', the land west of Andalusia.

When the light is right the scene in Tavira could be straight out of an old master painting. In the old town the streets are lined with the fine doorways and carved coats of arms that typify stately old Portuguese houses. The banks of the river are lined with fine gardens and cafés. Without really meaning to, the old town has managed to avoid tourism. It was once on the main road, the EN125, between southern Spain and southern Portugal, but found itself completely bypassed by the new motorway; not that anyone in Tavira is complaining.

Just five hundred yards from the town centre is the Convento de Santo António, founded in 1606 as a Capuchin friary. The monastic inhabitants grew medicinal herbs in the surrounding fields, which they dried and sold. The rest of the time was spent in meditation and prayer. Given the idyllic location, this lifestyle may not have been quite as much of a sacrifice as the order's founder intended. Inside, the building is a beautiful collection of cloisters and courtyards, all with skilfully constructed vaulted ceilings. Outside, the whitewashed compound detailed in touches of pale blue, dove grey and sunflower yellow looks out over the sea and the salt pans that distinguish this part of the Algarve. The fields have since been built over with rows of apartment buildings, but the view of the waters beyond is pretty much as it was.

If the area immediately surrounding the high walls of the friary has declined, the interiors have, if anything, improved. All the cloisters and vaulted ceilings have been immaculately preserved, while the sleeping accommodation is markedly better. Each bedroom was created from two of the cells in which the monks used to live. The monks certainly wouldn't have had antiques to

decorate their cells, nor en suite bathrooms, and definitely no swimming pool.

Modern luxuries aside, monasteries do make particularly good hotels, especially when they haven't been too tarted up. Not only do the massive walls ensure privacy and quiet, but they are very good insulation in a hot climate. The intricacy and finery of all those arches and vaulted ceilings makes most other forms of decoration redundant, encouraging a welcome simplicity of decor.

These monk's cells also make a great base for exploring the south of Portugal. You can go to the beach, walk to the old town, scour the countryside for painted peasant furniture, or linger all afternoon over lunch on the riverside. And however you choose to spend your days you will always have the tranquillity of the friary to return to. Once inside its walls, you can swim, read in the shade of a cloister or sunbake out in the courtyard, protected by the solitude and privacy that only a former monastery can provide. Perfectly divine.

---

address Convento de Santo António, Altalaia, 56–8800 Tavira, Algarve, Portugal
telephone (351) 281 325 632   **fax** (351) 282 321 573
room rates from 19 000 Escudos (including breakfast)

QUINTA
DE
S.ᵗᵒ ANTONIO

the gallery evason

A few years ago the saddest sight you were likely to see in Singapore was the handful of pale sweaty tourists in khaki shorts and sandals ordering gin and tonics in the rundown bar at the Raffles Hotel. Outside, young Singaporeans would be rushing about in their Armani suits meeting for cappuccinos in one of the supermodern shopping complexes, or joining each other for dinner in the never-ending choice of Singapore's air-conditioned hotels and restaurants. But inside, under the creaking ceiling fan, chipping paintwork, and crumbling walls of the Raffles Hotel bar, some Westerners were still playing 'pretend colonial'.

Raffles has now been completely renovated, but it remains an anomaly, an odd colonial low-rise amid a forest of high-tech high-rise. Let's be blunt: colonial Singapore is dead. Kaput. Finished. In its place is a thriving, fast-paced (and expensive) metropolis that many now consider the uncrowned capital of Asia. It has one of the largest and most modern airports, one of the busiest harbours, and one of the most comprehensive selections of designer-label shopping in the world. Singaporeans are affluent and eager to keep up with the latest trends in music, fashion, film and, of course, design.

It was only a matter of time then before Singapore got a hotel in keeping with its new, thoroughly modern status. Enter the Gallery Evason, located at one end of Mohammed Sultan Road, the grooviest street in the city. Singapore now finally has what most other world-class metropolises have – a hip hotel. Unlike other cities, however, where so many interesting hotels have been created within existing buildings, this one was custom built, like almost everything else in the new Singapore. Designed by William Lim Associates and Tangguanbee Architects, it is essentially an extension and refinement of some of their previous projects. The roof pool and metallic surfaces are reminiscent of Lim's apartment complex Paterson Edge, and the bold shots of colour and 3-D cutouts are typical of Tangguanbee's approach. Like Changi Airport, the scale is vast and the approach unashamedly bold. The three different block-shaped structures together with three stand-alone cylindrical glass silos house no less than 223 rooms, sixteen restaurants and bars, and a complete spa complex. And that's not all. There's a blue mosaic pool on the roof with glass sides, and a very popular night club on the ground floor.

The swimming pool, with glass sides and blue mosaic tiles, is cantilevered over the edge of the building

Dark timber, slick fixtures and fittings, and the odd splash of colour: the design is restrained but distinctively Asian

The bathrooms are defined by polished black granite floors, mosaic glass tiles and lots of shiny stainless steel

Bold colour is the ingredient that brings the design of Singapore's Gallery Evason to life

The restaurant tables are suspended from the soaring ceiling on stainless steel cables

Each room is amply equipped with a bar and provisions, all discreetly hidden behind a sliding panel of frosted glass

As far as I know, this is also the first major hotel to dedicate an entire floor to its single female guests, with elevator access carefully controlled. The idea is that the single female traveller will feel more protected (although in Singapore, a city with a virtually non-existent crime rate, it does seem a bit extreme). Most remarkable is that it is – by the exorbitant standards of this city – eminently affordable.

This is a hotel that is architecture-driven. The three different structures comprising the building mean that the rooms are of numerous different shapes and configurations. Some are square, some are elongated, some have window niches with settees, others have separate living spaces – but none suffer from the 'boring box' syndrome of many hotel rooms. The interior scheme is uniform, which feels logical given that the architecture is so varied. Every room has a bathroom in black granite and mosaic glass, a storage wall concealed behind frosted glass sliding screens, and a bed equipped with enough control buttons to drive a spaceship.

Journalists and commentators have described the Gallery Evason as minimal, but I'm inclined to disagree. I think the right word is functional – modern and functional. This is an ethos that pervades the details. It is embodied in the soft, low-level lighting that is programmed to come on automatically when you get out of bed to you save you stubbing your toes or bashing your shins; the air-conditioning regulated by one of the buttons behind your pillow; the special rack for your newspaper outside your door; or the internet television in every room.

Twenty-five years ago Singapore still had plenty of colonial cachet – but you had to have a haircut before you were allowed to enter the country. Times have changed. Now it's a thoroughly modern nation and you can wear your hair any way you like, any colour you like. The rickshaws, the satay stands and the colonial architecture have all but disappeared. In their place is a new vibrant modernism with a distinctly Asian metropolitan twist.

---

address   The Gallery Evason, 76 Robertson Quay #03–00, Singapore 238254

telephone (65) 849 8686   **fax** (65) 836 6666

room rates from Sing$295 (including breakfast)

parador de los reyes católicos

The Hostal de los Reyes Católicos is billed as the oldest hotel in the world. Founded in 1492 by King Ferdinand and Queen Isabella following their successful reconquest of Granada from the Moors, its imposing structure shares the main square of Santiago de Compostela with the soaring golden spires of the cathedral. Its purpose was to provide lodging for the pilgrims who walked here from all over Europe to pray at the cathedral's shrine of St James.

To Medieval Christians, Santiago ranked in importance with Jerusalem and Rome. Millions of Catholics would, at least once in their lifetime, walk the dusty and often dangerous pilgrim road across the Pyrenees mountains to this cathedral town located on Cabo Finisterre (literally 'cape at the end of the world' – exactly what it was until Columbus discovered the New World). In an age when church and state were profoundly interlinked, the pilgrimage was a source of great power and prestige for Ferdinand and Isabella's kingdom. They took a keen personal interest in the construction of this important building, and Queen Isabella herself ensured that it was supplied with the finest available materials and the best craftsmanship.

The pilgrimage to Santiago was not just an act of faith, it was one of the great adventures of its day. People dreamed of going to Santiago in the way that we might today dream of sailing around the world. It was an experience fraught with danger – it took money to make such a journey, and marauding bands of thieves and robbers knew it. And in the early Middle Ages, the final destination brought the devout Christian closer to the land of the Muslim infidel than anywhere else in Europe. Nonetheless, it was an adventure of a lifetime that took pilgrims past places and sights that they had likely never experienced before.

The pilgrim road was lined with castles that dominated every mountain pass, monasteries that opened their doors for overnight stays, and of course numerous Romanesque churches where the faithful would pray en route. However, there were also plenty of places where the pilgrims were left to fend for themselves against the weather, against the terrain and against the road pirates. In the mountains the best a traveller could hope for by way of shelter for the night was a *palloza*, a circular hut built of granite and topped with a conical thatched roof. Most were windowless with straw-covered floors and bare stone walls.

These round dwellings are one of the oldest surviving building types in Europe, with roots in the Bronze Age. They were low, dark and smelly too, for they also sheltered animals. But even today, many of these surviving *pallozas* have been set aside as *refugios* for young pilgrims walking to Santiago (minus the animals, of course).

Yes, although most people are probably entirely unaware of it, the pilgrimage still takes place. Shirley MacLaine – film star, New Age evangelist, and sister of Warren Beatty – is one of the more high-profile people recently to have completed what is still, by her own account, an adventure and an ordeal. If you can forgive the 'in my previous life' mumbo jumbo, her book *El Camino* makes an interesting read, for it highlights how little the route has changed since the Middle Ages.

The destination of pilgrims was and is Santiago de Compostela, a university town that's every bit as engaging today as it was in the Middle Ages, although for vastly different reasons. The narrow lanes and alleys of the well-preserved old quarter are now crammed with interesting little bars and restaurants, but the Hostal de los Reyes Católicos, five hundred years on, is still *the* place to stay. Combining jaw-dropping history with very welcome affordability, it is part of the government-run programme of Paradores, a successful rescue plan for Spain's wonderful collection of historic castles, forts and monasteries. With its four courtyards named after the evangelists, its soaring public spaces filled with majestic tapestries and imposing antiques, and its vast bedrooms with their four-poster beds, the hotel could be the setting for a remake of *El Cid*.

A cinematic reference is not entirely inappropriate given that just across the Plaza do Obradoiro is the magnificent Santiago Cathedral. Its famously gigantic silver censor, known as a *botafumeiro*, featured memorably in Ridley Scott's *1492: Conquest of Paradise* as it swung eerily along the full length of the cathedral transept.

address Parador de los Reyes Católicos, Plaza do Obradoiro #1, 15705 Santiago de Compostela, Spain

telephone (34) 0981 582 200   **fax** (34) 0981 563 094

room rates from 21,200 Pesetas

birger jarl

In Sweden they do things differently. Everything is infused with a disciplined design sense. Even the salt and pepper sachets on Scandinavian airlines get the Nordic treatment. Salt is blue, pepper is red; there is no text on either packet except for a quote on the pepper sachet, which reads: 'Pepper is a gift from the Orient – but gift means poison in Swedish' (huh?). They are undoubtedly the best-looking salt and pepper sachets on any airline. The same goes for the hand towel, the headrest and the coffee cup. Even the in-flight shopping guide is, for once, full of things I would like to buy – and not only that but when you order they also have the things in stock. There is something very satisfying about the efficiency, precision and acute aesthetic sensibility of the Scandinavian mentality.

The new Birger Jarl is the perfect expression of that mentality. When Yvonne Sörensen took over as managing director of this huge 1970s property, it was really beginning to show its age. She was determined not just to restore it but to create something new and distinctive – and distinctively Swedish. She decided to incorporate Swedish colour, form and contemporary design in its refurbishment. Thus twelve of Sweden's best-known designers

were approached and each invited to put their individual stamp on one of the guest rooms.

Twelve rooms from a total of 240 is not exactly numerically significant, but they provided a start on which the hotel plans to build and, more importantly, they set the tone for the rest of the renovation. Even so, I was wary. Some of the rooms depicted in the brochure looked a bit Ikea-ish to me, and I was not expecting anything outstanding. But the Swedish approach to design is more subtle, less showy. It's an aesthetic that grows on you slowly instead of sweeping you off your feet. As with those SAS salt and pepper sachets, the more you look, the more you notice. Each of the individually designed rooms is equipped with a large, recently released volume on Swedish design, and as you flick through, you soon recognize the lights, tables, chairs, and even the rubbish bins. It's worth reading about the ideas behind some of these design schemes too. The corner suite by Jonas Bohlin, one of Swedish design's biggest names, was inspired by a journey he made from Sweden to France in a small wooden rowing boat. Along the way, he invited different personalities to accompany him and those that did received a pair of numbered, signed, beautifully handmade oars.

Johanna Köhlin and Agneta Pettersson
are two young Swedish designers who
use light as a decorative ingredient

The room designed by Eva Lilja
Löwenhielm and Anya Sebton is very
nordic and very minimal

Fern green and arctic white are among
the colours and themes of Sweden that
recur throughout the hotel

A very seventies silk-screened forest
scene curtains the window of the
Löwenhielm and Sebton-designed room

Strong shapes and dark colours define
the design signature of experienced
Swedish hotel architect Franz Hardinger

Fishing net or tutu? Whatever the
inspiration, Jonas Bohlin stands out in
the current Swedish design scene

The contrast of dark and light
distinguishes the room designed by
Franz Hardinger

A detail of the decor in the 'Miss Dottie'
room designed by Thomas Sandell

Sandell's 'Mr Glad' suite has a single
wall in vibrant orange and an eclectic
selection of contemporary furniture

The newest, most recently renovated 'Standard' rooms at Birger Jarl feature painted walls by select Swedish artists

Blue and white stripes are typical of this classic Swedish room recently created by design firm Svenskt Tenn

Twelve rooms were created by individual designers, but even the so-called 'Standard' rooms are anything but

Swedish poems on fabric panels are the latest addition to some of the 'Standard' rooms at Birger Jarl

Johan Stylander's design makes reference to his new metropolitan base in New York

The bar is separated from the restaurant by a massive frosted green glass screen etched with polka dots

Blond beech wood on white walls sets the light-filled, distinctly Scandinavian tone of one specially commissioned suite

White room – black bathroom. The tiles are part of Johan Stylander's sophisticated design

The suite created by designers at the classic Swedish company Svenskt Tenn is in a more folk-influenced style

Not only does this make sense of the oars hanging on the walls, but it also gives depth and context to Bohlin's evident respect for natural materials such as traditionally tanned leathers and blond untreated timbers.

There is an artistic resonance to the interiors at Birger Jarl, and much to be learned about Swedish design. There are rooms that sport a sauna-esque minimalism and others splattered with Nordic polka dots. In fact all twelve designed rooms are completely different in all but one respect: light. Scandinavia may be the land of the midnight sun but it's also notorious for its long dark winters. Maximizing daylight was a priority throughout. But what, you might ask, are those 228 standard rooms like? The cynic might suspect that twelve rooms were 'tarted up' to generate publicity and custom for the other 228 bland ones. That, however, would not be fair. Swedish design pervades the entire hotel. Blond timber and the red of Swedish barns and farms combine in the lobby with green glass and stainless steel.

Guest rooms are predominantly white with the odd tint of green. Birger Jarl is modern and spacious, but not in the theatrical way of some city hotels. Sober is the word that keeps coming to mind in Scandinavia.

Stockholm itself, however, could certainly not be described as sober. It is the Barcelona of the north, a vibrant cosmopolitan destination that combines the handsome architecture of one of the Baltic's most historic cities with a charming setting on an archipelago of islands. The city has a bubbling vitality and the streets are full of jazz bars, live music venues, and unusual little restaurants. Birger Jarl is in a district known as Little Asia. Thai, Japanese, Chinese, Vietnamese, even Cuban restaurants literally surround the hotel. Stockholm has a real buzz to it right now. But even the most ardent urban adventurer needs a room to come back to, and at Birger Jarl – in the words of designers Eva Lilja Löwenhielm and Anya Sebton – it's a 'soothing room with Nordic materials and Nordic feelings.'

---

address Hotel Birger Jarl, Box 190 16, Tulegatan 8, 104 32 Stockholm, Sweden

telephone (46) 8 674 18 00   **fax** (46) 8 673 73 66

room rates from 1,287 Krona

pansea ksar ghilane

Not so long ago it would have seemed slightly odd to choose the Sahara Desert as a holiday destination. Now, with a global consumer culture quickly erasing the differences between one place and the next, people are starting to look further afield for adventure and discovery. The Sahara Desert has joined the Amazon and the Arctic as a travel destination, and the term 'going to extremes' has acquired a whole new meaning – a literal one.

As desert experiences go, Pansea may qualify as the purest. The main attraction – the only attraction – is sand. Red sand, ochre sand, pale sand, rocky sand – think of every desert movie you've ever seen and you can picture it. (This, for example, is where they filmed *The English Patient*.) Pansea is not near the desert, or on the fringe of the desert, it's well and truly *in* it. This oasis tent town, described rather succinctly in French as *Nomade Deluxe*, can only be reached by four-wheel drive through soft dunes of sand so powdery that you sink to your knees. You could travel via Tozeur, an ancient and spectacular oasis of 200,000 palm trees that was once a Roman outpost and is now world-renowned for its dates. Or you might come direct from Djerba, three hours away on the coast. The last stop before casting

off for the sand is the outpost town of Douz, a place that was a gateway to the desert long before adventure travel became commercialized. Thankfully, tourism has changed none of the town's time-honoured traditions. Thursday is market day, and nomads arrive to trade camels, horses, craft, woven blankets, richly adorned saddles and silver jewelry. It's a more atmospheric place to buy a rug than Djerba, even if the choice is more limited. From Douz, the Sahara safaris depart for the exotically named Great Erg Oriental, a vast multi-coloured ocean of soft waves of sand. Pansea Ksar Ghilane is nestled in its own oasis in the middle of the Erg.

They say you can only truly appreciate an oasis after having crossed a desert, and they're right. Pansea's oasis arrives just at the point when you start to wonder whether this may be your last adventure – ever. It is, to put it mildly, a most welcome and refreshing break from the unrelenting heat. The tents, pitched under palm trees, are vast, with every amenity you could wish for, including en suite bathrooms, and (thank Allah) air conditioning. With three hundred square feet of floor space, they're not exactly your average tent, but then nor is Pansea your average camp. Facilities such as a restaurant and a cigar bar are housed in a tall stone tower modelled on a *ksar*, a traditional Berber granary. The guest tents are also impressive. Their style is simple but with sophisticated detailing. The air-conditioning vent, for example, is hidden behind a screen of *moushrabiya*, the traditional Arabic wooden grilles carved with complex geometric patterns.

It may come as a surprise to learn that these tents were devised by a Brussels-based architectural firm, Atlante, but in fact Olivier de Mot and Jean-François Lehembre have made a name as architects of tents. They did it for Amanwana on Moyo Island; here they have done it for an island of a different type, an island in the sand. Specialists they may be in the design of tents, credited with technical innovations like a ventilating double roof, but at Pansea they still had to cope with the sand that blows into every crack and crevice and through every slit. It's a battle as old as time and for a while it looked like the sand would win. The pool was in danger of becoming a

sand pit until they designed a retaining fence from woven green palm fronds.

Welcome or not, sand is the number one ingredient of the Ksar Ghilane experience. Dunes stretch in every direction, as far as the eye can see. They make this a place of mystery and silence and – rather more unexpectedly – a place of action. The dunes are a perfect venue for racing in dune buggies à la Paris-Dakar, or for skimming just above the ground in ultra-light aircraft. Short of the one tower back in camp, there's nothing to run into. For the more traditionally inclined, there's always the option of pounding along in the heat on the back of a temperamental and uncomfortable desert beast, though personally I wouldn't recommend it.

The adventure ends where it started – Djerba, an island of ten thousand palms rising out of the Mediterranean, with Roman ruins, centuries-old olive orchards, open-air markets, the oldest synagogue in the world, and – dare I say it – fine sand beaches.

---

address Pansea Ksar Ghilane, Ksar Ghilane, Governora de Kebili, Tunisia
telephone (216) 5 621870 **fax** (216) 5 621872
room rates from 98 Tun. Dhs

the albion

Every morning it's the same story. Enormous motor homes converted into mobile closets with changing rooms line up outside the entrance to the Albion. The lobby briefly churns into a whirlwind of activity: the crew, the photographers, the assistants, the stylists, the make-up artists, the location scouts, the ubiquitous client's representative, and of course the models (easy to spot – they're the ones who always look like they need another night's sleep) – all of them leave this pared-down Art Deco gem and pile into their home for the day. They are always in a hurry and always late. This is early morning soap – live! – a mobile, tropical version of *The Bold and the Beautiful*.

The photoshoot is booming business in Miami. This is the city of choice for Dutch, German, French, English, Scandinavian, Italian and even American retailing giants when it comes to photographing their catalogues and campaigns. The sunshine is dependable and the photography business well-established, with an infrastructure that includes labs, equipment hire, studios, and of course those ubiquitous 'location vehicles'. All of that makes it more efficient and less expensive to travel here than to try and make Hamburg or Frankfurt look like an exotic location in the dead of winter.

If Miami is currently one of the world's most popular photoshoot locations, the Albion is currently the most popular hotel for photo crews – and not just because fashion people would rather die than stay in the wrong place. Photoshoots have budgets too, and the bottom line, no matter how hip the place, is whether it is affordable. The Albion, the latest creation of brother and sister duo Jason and Jennifer Rubell, is one of the first of Miami's Hip Hotels to bridge the gap between style and price. Rooms are elegant, generous, and sparely furnished with the odd sculptural piece by Carlos Zapata, the avant-garde Ecuadorean architect who oversaw the building's renovation. Bathrooms are equally simple: all white with a counter in brushed stainless steel. The ingredient that is thankfully allowed to dominate throughout is the architecture – the original architecture. Designed in 1939 by Igor Polivitsky, renowned architect of the Hotel Nacional in Havana, the building is like a sleek ocean liner marooned on a street corner just one block back from the beach. Punctuated with large round windows that have the exaggerated appearance of portholes, it is straight out of Miami's glamour days. Just a glance at the lobby will tell you that.

The blue-green portholes looking into the pool from the garden are perhaps the Albion's single most unusual feature

Everywhere you look, exquisite details testify to the building's significant Art Deco credentials

Architecturally, the Albion remains true to Igor Polivitsky's original scheme; only the decor and design were renewed

The facade is a vivid reminder of South Beach's Art Deco-inspired building boom in the 1930s

Architect Carlos Zapata designed everything, including the visually disconcerting, leaning chairs

Much the most unusual rooms are the sky courtyard suites: a living room and a bedroom linked by an open-air terrace

the albion

This towering, triple-storey space is enhanced by what the Rubells describe as a 'vertical pond' (a 600-square-foot waterfall), and its sculpted ceilings are supported by tall slender columns shaped like gigantic flower stems. But the outstanding feature of this Art Deco gem has to be the 'solarium suites' on the top floor. Very bright, very white, with an amazing view and a huge amount of space, each of these mini-apartments is built around a penthouse courtyard, an outdoor room perfect for private sun-baking *au naturel* or an *al fresco* breakfast.

The Miami heritage authorities must be very happy with the Rubells. The Albion today looks just as it does in 1930s photos, yet it took the princely sum of ten million dollars to rescue it from years of indifference. And unlike the recently completed National Hotel around the corner – which although celebrated as an accurate renovation actually feels rather old-fashioned – the Albion does not suffer from nostalgia. The Rubells were not interested in simply recreating history. The interior of the

Albion is new and different, but in a manner that harmonizes with the original features. The way the space is used reflects the very modern and relaxed attitude of the hotel. Instead of a full kitchen there's a cold food pantry that serves breakfasts, sandwiches and salads twenty-four hours a day. The hotel's café (which shares the pantry menu) is on the mezzanine looking down into the spectacular lobby (and so is a perfect place to witness those unfolding photo-crew dramas). The pool, immediately off the mezzanine café, is higher than the lobby and is dotted with glass portholes that give a glimpse of the swimmers within. And the bar, the surreal Fallabella Bar, is a sculptural hodgepodge of odd angles in glass, aluminium and plywood.

The Albion combines the avant-garde edge of South Beach design with the glamour of one of its original Art Deco architectural pearls – at a price significantly lower than, say, the Delano. So spend the money you save on a 'solarium suite' … it's worth it.

address The Albion, 1650 James Avenue at Lincoln Road, Miami Beach, FL 33139, USA
telephone (1) 305 913 10 00 **fax** (1) 305 674 05 07
room rates from US$155

the greenview

When it opened in January 1995, the Greenview was the first new hotel for decades in the Lincoln Road area of Miami's South Beach, then still derelict and virtually unaffected by the runaway success and runaway prices of Ocean Drive. This 1939 Art Deco hotel had been shuttered for eight years. Its relaunch by Jennifer and Jason Rubell was a pioneering move in the fast-paced renovation race that consumed South Beach in the 1990s. It was followed, a year later, by the much ballyhooed opening of Ian Schrager's Delano Hotel around the corner. The niece and nephew of Steve Rubell were now officially in competition with their uncle's former business partner, albeit with a totally different agenda.

If the Delano is for people looking to be entertained, the Greenview is for people who know how to make their own fun. For if there is such a thing as your basic Hip Hotel, then this is it. The Greenview has no frills, just simple good style. The rooms, for example, are invitingly spare. Bare wooden floors, a woven sisal rug, a white Bertoia chair in the corner, pale blue walls, white linen, blond timber vanity table, white Venetian blinds: it's a cool, calm composition, perfect for a hot climate and for people (like me) who don't get on with air conditioning. No doubt more than one guest has gone home and copied the formula for their own apartment. And why not? No single ingredient is particularly expensive, but the restrained, considered manner in which Parisian designer Chahan Minassian put it all together makes it more than worthy of imitation.

The Greenview has an equally sparse and elegant lobby, where a Continental-style buffet breakfast (included in the rate) is served all morning. The atmosphere is casually relaxed, and although there are quite a few hotels in South Beach that perhaps offer more luxury and glamour, the Greenview has a fiercely loyal following. In this sense it's a lot like a small European hotel. Once people feel comfortable, and a few nights don't break the bank, they see no reason to change. The big drawcard is style … and price. But it's not just restricted budgets that bring them here, for these are people who would rather spend their money on going out. And from the Greenview that's easy to do.

Situated two blocks back from the beach, the hotel is across the street from the Lincoln Road pedestrian mall, described by US *Travel & Leisure* magazine as 'another glamorous symbol of the new, grown-up South Beach'.

If only all malls in the US were like this! Home of the New World Symphony and the Miami City Ballet, Lincoln Road is adorned with fancifully decorative Art Deco buildings, mosaic floors, reflecting pools, concrete sculptures, experimental theatres, sidewalk cafés, palm trees, influential galleries, famous restaurants, new shops, lots of roller bladers and even a picturesque Mission church. By night all of Lincoln Road becomes a veritable sea of candlelit tables. This sexy little strip is fast becoming the more adventurous alternative to Ocean Drive.

Once again, for the second time in a century, Lincoln Road has become one of the hottest streets in Miami. In its heyday it was known as the Fifth Avenue of the South, the Florida address of big-name department stores such as Saks Fifth Avenue and I Magnin. It was also home to some glamorous cinemas, which regularly held glittering Hollywood-style premieres. But the 1950s arrival of the 'American Plan', the first package holiday deal,

brought about the slow but inexorable decline of Lincoln Road. Innocently enough, the American Plan offered the tourist so many inclusive extras that hotels became hermetically self-contained – places not just for guests to eat and sleep but to get their entertainment as well. This cut deeply into the local nightclub, cinema and restaurant trade. Shops inside these big hotels similarly hurt local retailers. Even the half-million-dollar conversion by famed architect Morris Lapidus of 'posh Lincoln' into a pedestrian mall in 1960 could not halt the decay. Saks was the last big name to leave (in the 1960s) and by the early 1980s Lincoln was lined with abandoned storefronts. It was a derelict dump colonized by drug dealers.

But it still had good bones. Now, after a concentrated, two-year, seventeen-million-dollar facelift, the reflecting pools, fountains and landscaped walkways are back to their former glory, and Lincoln is once again one of the most beautiful promenades in America.

---

address The Greenview, 1671 Washington Avenue, Miami, FL 33139, USA

telephone (1) 305 531 6588   **fax** (1) 305 531 4580

room rates from US$100

the standard

Sunset Strip is where the Hollywood legend began. All the scandal and the intrigue that has so captivated the popular press for the past seventy-odd years started in the bars, clubs and hotels on Sunset. In the thirties and forties, it was the Mocambo and the Tropicana that pulled the stars and kickstarted the celebrity cult. The fifties brought Sinatra and his Rat Pack, who were regulars at Ciro's, along with the likes of Marilyn Monroe and Jayne Mansfield. Over the years places closed and places opened, but the Strip endured as *the* place for the famous and the would-be famous to hang out. Even the total change of the sixties – with new attitudes, new freedoms and new fashions – did not derail the Strip. Quite the opposite. Jim Morrison and the Doors, Sonny and Cher, Frank Zappa, and Mammas and the Papas were all discovered at a hot new club on Sunset called the Whisky.

The Mocambo and the Tropicana are long defunct, but the Strip is as relevant as it always was. These days the places to hang out and be seen are hotels. At one end of Sunset Boulevard near the corner of La Cienega is the Mondrian, an all-white favourite with the music crowd – the *established* music crowd. At the other end there is the legendary Chateau Marmont, firm

favourite with the film crowd – the *established* film crowd. In between the two is the brash new upstart, the Standard.

The name is ironic, for it is anything but. The crowd that jam the bar every night is from the worlds of music and film, but they are younger and hungrier, less set in their ways. The Standard is perfect for them and vice versa. It was created for precisely this young clientele, sophisticated in taste but limited in means. This was a niche specifically identified by André Balazs, hotel entrepreneur and proprietor of successful Hip Hotels like Chateau Marmont down the road and the Mercer in New York.

The Standard was not, however, simply a matter of scaling down the ingredients of his other properties. It is a project driven more by attitude than by design concept. It turns convention on its head at every possible opportunity (including the upside-down logo). The only shop in the lobby is Ed's Barber Shop, with the slogan: 'no nicks or cheap cuts' (they also do the odd tattoo). The lobby contains a glass vitrine where a nightly work of performance art is staged in the form of a scantily clad girl reading a book or sleeping in full view of those checking in or out.

ANY JAIL
ANY COURT
ANY TIME
(323) 464-8484
http//www.hollywoodbailbonds.com

blow

harder   hard

stop

The shag-pile carpet in the lobby runs up the wall and onto the ceiling, and the pool deck is surfaced in blue astroturf. The controls for the air-conditioning irreverently read 'blow hard' and 'blow harder'. The bar features a wall-to-wall desertscape mural of a kind last seen (some might say thankfully) in the seventies. The matches – especially the matches – sum it all up. In four surfer fluorescent shades they promote 'Hollywood Bail Bonds', unashamedly proclaiming 'you're only one call away from freedom – anyone, any jail, any time'. If you happen to be part of a new band intent on having a good time, this place is it, and the matches might provide more than a laugh.

But do not be misled by all the irreverence. Behind the Standard's bag of tricks there are very sound foundations. The beds are identical to those in Chateau Marmont, the pillows are down-filled, and each room is equipped with a personal stereo system and a squillion channels on a widescreen state-of-the-art TV. The phone jacks are for internet access and offer high-speed ISDN connections, and the hotel is fully equipped with business facilities, including a funky conference room (even if most guests don't know it). On the design front too, there's plenty of pedigree. The arched lamps in the lobby are Italian classics by Achille Castiglioni, lamps in the diner-restaurant are by Alvar Aalto and the overall scheme was inspired by Gio Ponti. The curtain fabric is an Andy Warhol print, for which the hotel had to seek special permission from his estate. Even the orange bathroom tiles are a re-edition of an American classic, and the loos themselves are – well of course – by American Standard. None of the ingredients, however, were meant to be viewed separately. It's the mixing of all these funky details and design classics that makes the Standard such an unusual hotel experience.

Originally built in 1963, this hotel used to be called the Thunderbird. The slogan of the Thunderbirds TV series was 'Thunderbirds are go'. Add another 'go' and the slogan works perfectly for the Standard.

address The Standard, 8300 Sunset Boulevard, Hollywood, CA 90069, USA
telephone (1) 323 650 9090 **fax** (1) 323 650 2820
room rates from US$99

the wawbeek

New York high society didn't always escape to the Hamptons. A hundred years ago the majestic Adirondack Mountains were the preferred retreat. With their lakes, beaches and cool forests – a welcome respite from New York's heat and humidity in summer – and their pristine ice and snow in winter, the Adirondacks were an established part of the seasonal society escape. But it wasn't just the summer climate or the spectacular beauty that made the Adirondacks so popular; they were given an additional boost by property developer Thomas Durant, who made the mountains accessible to city folk by building the Adirondack railway line, completed in 1871.

Even so, it was a few years before Durant, or rather his son William, caught the attention of New York's millionaires. In 1879, William Durant showed the rich something really fantastical they could do with their money. He commissioned an incredibly elaborate and luxurious compound in this wilderness destination built largely out of unskinned logs. The idea swiftly caught on. It was the first 'great camp', and soon every tycoon just had to have one. These baroque creations in logs were very grand, very eccentric, and very expensive. For the first time, American money had found

its own equivalent of the Alpine *Schloss*. Builders of the great camps set out not only to copy but to outdo the aristocratic splendour of a European castle in the snow. They had enormous fireplaces built in riverstone, chandeliers made from antlers, bearskin rugs and countless hunting trophies (shot or bought – it didn't matter, so long as it was impressive.) The grandest of all the great camps was, appropriately enough, built by the richest man in America, William Avery Rockefeller. Logs were used to construct everything from a private service station and a boathouse for an entire fleet of boats to a formal dining room with a thirty foot ceiling and a monumental riverstone fireplace at either end.

Today, Rockefeller's camp on Lake Saranac thrives as an exclusive hotel called the Point. It's a sensational place with equally sensational levels of luxury and, of course, a price tag to match. As a hotel experience, it is largely limited to mini-Rockefellers. On the very same lake however, in an equally idyllic location, is another great camp that offers the same enchanting log cabin experience at far more affordable rates. The Wawbeek, on Upper Saranac Lake, is the real thing – a turn-of-the-century forty-acre property that features both individual log cabins and spacious rooms in a larger Lake House. Its interiors have abundant fireplaces, endless cosy nooks for reading, and plenty of antler lamps and hunting trophies. In addition to the two living rooms packed with card tables, games, books, and cushion-filled corners (but no TVs – anywhere), most of the rooms in the Lake House have their own fireside sitting areas. The views across lake and mountains are magnificent. It's a homely aesthetic designed to allow the stressed-out New Yorker to regain some balance of life.

Even so, the best place to be is outdoors. As the locals say, 'here in the north country, all seasons are intense.' Walk, hike, swim, bike, and sail in the summer (all gear is included in the price, by the way) and cross-country ski, skate, snow-shoe and fish in the winter. There's even downhill skiing not far away. The nearest mountain is Big Tupper, only eight miles from the Wawbeek, and thirty miles away is Lake Placid, the venue for not one but two Winter Olympics. For some just the air and the unspoiled natural beauty of the place is stimulus enough.

Active or not, all guests have the food to look forward to in the evening. The Wawbeek restaurant, located in the camp's original dining cabin on a rocky promontory overlooking the lake, has a considerable culinary reputation. Chef Richard Brosseau has brought international city standards to the Adirondacks, and anyone who has eaten at the Wawbeek will be grateful that he did. That said, the food is not inappropriate to the setting. The menu is entirely in step with the outdoor life, offering hearty, meaty dishes like Roasted Pheasant Breast, Roasted Long Island Free-Range Duck or Greek-Marinated and Grilled Lamb Steak. And don't miss the wild wintergreen ice cream dessert.

A 'great camp' is a great experience; a great camp with great food at a great price is an even better one.

---

address The Wawbeek, 55 Panther Mountain Road, Rt. 30 Upper Saranac Lake, Tupper Lake, NY 12986, USA

telephone (1) 518 359 2656 (1 800 953 2656)   **fax** (1) 518 359 2475

room rates from US$129 (including breakfast and use of boats)

First published in paperback in the United States of America in 2001 by Thames & Hudson Inc., 500 Fifth Avenue, New York, New York 10110

Library of Congress Catalog Card Number 2001086845

ISBN 0-500-28302-8

Designed by Maggi Smith

Printed and bound in Singapore by CS Graphics

Photography by Herbert Ypma, with the exception of La Aldea and Eivindsplass Fjellgard, by Mirjam Bleeker/Taverne Agency (styling for Eivindsplass Fjellgard by Frank Visser/Taverne Agency); Portixol, by Hotze Eisma/Taverne Agency; Les Terrasses and La Tortuga, by Hans Zeegers/Taverne Agency; Parador de los Reyes Católicos, courtesy of Paradores de Turisme de España; Pansea Ksar Ghilane, courtesy of Pansea Hotels and Resorts. Portrait of John Malkovich (p. 94) by Jon Mortimer, courtesy of the Big Sleep Hotel.